INCORPORATING CLIMATE RESILIENCE IN URBAN PLANNING AND POLICY MAKING

FOCUS ON ARMENIA, GEORGIA, AND UZBEKISTAN

AUGUST 2023

ASIAN DEVELOPMENT BANK

ADB

© 2023 Asian Development Bank
6 ADB Avenue, Mandaluyong City, 1550 Metro Manila, Philippines
Tel +63 2 8632 4444; Fax +63 2 8636 2444
www.adb.org

Some rights reserved. Published in 2023.

ISBN 978-92-9270-253-3 (print); 978-92-9270-254-0 (electronic); 978-92-9270-255-7 (e-book)
Publication Stock No. SPR230279-2
DOI: http://dx.doi.org/10.22617/SPR230279-2

The views expressed in this publication are those of the authors and do not necessarily reflect the views and policies of the Asian Development Bank (ADB) or its Board of Governors or the governments they represent.

ADB does not guarantee the accuracy of the data included in this publication and accepts no responsibility for any consequence of their use. The mention of specific companies or products of manufacturers does not imply that they are endorsed or recommended by ADB in preference to others of a similar nature that are not mentioned.

By making any designation of or reference to a particular territory or geographic area, or by using the term "country" in this publication, ADB does not intend to make any judgments as to the legal or other status of any territory or area.

Please contact pubsmarketing@adb.org if you have questions or comments with respect to content, or if you wish to obtain copyright permission for your intended use that does not fall within these terms, or for permission to use the ADB logo.

Corrigenda to ADB publications may be found at http://www.adb.org/publications/corrigenda.

Notes:
In this publication, "$" refers to United States dollars.
The boundaries or any other information shown on the maps in this publication do not imply any judgment by ADB on the legal status of any territory, or any endorsement or acceptance of such boundaries or information.

On the cover: Changing climate conditions are threatening the fragile ecosystems and natural and built environments of Armenia, Georgia, and Uzbekistan. "Zoo Animals Escape Flooding in Tbilisi, Georgia" (photo by katexic is licensed under CC BY 2.0).

Other photos are from the ADB Multimedia Library.
Cover design by Jan Carlo Dela Cruz.

CONTENTS

TABLES AND FIGURES

Figures

FOREWORD

The changing climate is threatening the fragile ecosystems of Armenia, Georgia, and Uzbekistan. It also threatens their built environments, compounding challenges of rapid urbanization and environmental degradation. Proactive adaptive urban planning is essential to reduce and manage climate risk, but this requires adequate data on climate trends and projections, and comprehensive analyses of climate hazards, exposure, vulnerability, and potential impacts.

This publication provides urban climate risk assessments at the national level, and for selected cities in Armenia, Georgia, and Uzbekistan. The results of these assessments have been developed into climate risk profiles to help mainstream climate resilience in urban planning and management, and to support government investment decisions and policy making in line with nationally determined contributions and adaptation plans.

Findings from these climate risk assessments are helping to integrate low-carbon and climate resilience measures into the planning and design of priority urban projects. The assessment for Georgia contributed to new investments by the Asian Development Bank (ADB) in the Sustainable Water Supply and Sanitation Sector Development Program and the Livable Cities Investment Project. Meanwhile, the assessment for Uzbekistan informed the design of the Integrated Urban Development Project, which will support inclusive, resilient, and sustainable infrastructure and services in four secondary cities. Lessons and good practices from this project will be replicated in other cities in Uzbekistan.

For ADB, boosting support for climate resilience in urban and water projects is part of a holistic approach to scaling up investments in adaptation. This is key to delivering on the third operational priority of ADB's Strategy 2030: tackling climate change, building climate and disaster resilience, and enhancing environmental sustainability. In 2021, ADB announced its ambition to deliver $100 billion of climate finance from 2019 to 2030, of which $34 billion will be allocated for investments in adaptation.

We hope that these urban climate assessments, along with their recommendations, help government stakeholders place climate change at the forefront of their decision-making, facilitate policy dialogues, and promote strategic planning on adaptation opportunities for enhanced resilience.

Bruno Carrasco
Director General
Climate Change and Sustainable Development Department

Yevgeniy Zhukov
Director General
Central and West Asia Department

ACKNOWLEDGMENTS

This publication was developed by a One ADB project team, composed mainly of sector and thematic specialists from the Water and Urban Development Sector Office (SG-WUD), Sectors Group; and the Climate Change, Resilience, and Environment Cluster (CCRE), Climate Change and Sustainable Development Department (CCSD). It aims to assist urban focal agencies, ADB project teams, and development practitioners in incorporating climate resilience in urban planning and policy making. The high-level climate risk assessments and recommendations it provides harness the prevailing climate data, models and projections, and state-of-the-art methodology in risk mapping, combining a suite of hazard, exposure, and vulnerability layers, and relevant adaptation measures and policies in each of the countries covered.

We would like to thank the following ADB senior staff who acted as advisors for the project: **Yong Ye**, Country Director, Pakistan, and former Director, Urban Development and Water Division of the Central and West Asia Department (CWRD); **Nianshan Zhang**, Head, Office of Safeguards (OSFG), and former Senior Advisor, CWRD; **Preety Bhandari**, former Director, Climate Change and Disaster Risk Management Division (SDCD), Sustainable Development and Climate Change (SDCC); **Noelle O'Brien**, Director, Climate Change, CCRE; and **Manoj Sharma**, Director, Water and Urban Development, SG-WUD. We would also like to thank the following ADB staff for contributing to the development of the profiles: **Paolo Spantigati**, Advisor, Office of the Director General, CWRD, and former Country Director, Armenia; **Shane Rosenthal**, Regional Director, Pacific Liaison and Coordination Office in Sydney, Australia (PLCO), Pacific Department (PARD), and former Country Director, Georgia; **Enrico Pinali**, Regional Head (Private Sector Development), Private Sector Development Unit, CWRD, and former Officer-in-Charge, Uzbekistan Resident Mission; **Neeta Pokhrel**, Director, Water and Urban Development, SG-WUD; **Heeyoung Hong**, Principal Urban Development Specialist, SG-WUD; and **Nathan Rive**, Senior Climate Change Specialist, CCRE. Finally, we would like to convey our appreciation to the CWRD, CCRE, CCSD, and Department of Communications and Knowledge Management staff, consultants, and pool of artists and service providers who saw through the production of this publication.

Team Leaders

Xijie Lu, *Urban Development Specialist, SG-WUD*
Kate Hughes, *Principal Climate Change Specialist, CCRE*
Malte Maass, *Climate Change Specialist, CCRE*
Maria Pia Ancora, *Senior Urban Development Specialist, SG-WUD*
Ramola Naik Singru, *Principal Urban Development Specialist, SG-WUD*
Ron Slangen, *Deputy Country Director, Viet Nam Resident Mission*

Peer Reviewers

Alessio Giardino, *Senior Water Specialist (Climate Change), CCRE*
Belinda Hewitt, *Senior Disaster Risk Management Specialist, CCRE*
Stefan Rau, *Principal Urban Development Specialist, SG-WUD*
Virinder Sharma, *former Principal Urban Development Specialist, Urban Sector Group, SDCC*
Vivian Castro-Wooldridge, *former Senior Urban Development Specialist, Urban Development and Water Division, PARD*

Consultants

Jack Beard, *FutureWater*
Peter Droogers, *FutureWater*
Arthur Lutz, *FutureWater*
Casper Van der Tak
Malkhaz Adeishvili
Arsen Karapetyan

ABBREVIATIONS AND SYMBOLS

Abbreviations

ADB	Asian Development Bank
DMC	developing member country
GCM	global circulation model
mm	millimeter
NASA	National Aeronautics and Space Administration
NASA-NEX	NASA Earth Exchange
NDC	nationally determined contribution
O&M	operation and maintenance
RCP	representative concentration pathway
SUDS	sustainable urban drainage system

Symbols

Δ	change
>	greater than

GLOSSARY

▶ ERA5 refers to the fifth-generation atmospheric reanalysis of the global climate covering January 1950 to the present. Produced by the Copernicus Climate Change Service at the European Centre for Medium-Range Weather Forecasts, it provides hourly estimates of many atmospheric, land, and oceanic climate variables.

▶ Global circulation models (GCMs) represent physically based, three-dimensional models that simulate atmospheric and oceanic processes to generate predictions of future large-scale climate trends. They have been demonstrated to reproduce observed features of recent and past climate change. Therefore, there is confidence that they can provide credible estimates of future climate change, particularly at continental and larger scales.

▶ Representative concentration pathways (RCPs) are scenarios that include time series of emissions and concentrations of the full suite of greenhouse gases (GHGs), aerosols, and chemically active gases. They are used to predict how GHG concentrations will change because of human activities, with RCP85 representing a high emissions scenario and RCP45 representing a medium emissions scenario.

▶ Return period indicates the period in years in which a hazard is likely to occur based on historical record.

BACKGROUND AND STRUCTURE OF THE REPORT

Under the 2015 Paris Agreement, countries communicate their nationally determined contributions (NDCs), which define targets, measures, and policies to reduce greenhouse gas emissions and adapt to the adverse effects of climate change. To help its developing member countries (DMCs) achieve their climate commitments, the Asian Development Bank (ADB) has elevated its ambition to deliver climate financing to its DMCs to $100 billion from 2019 to 2030.[1] Under Strategy 2030,[2] ADB has committed to align 75% of its operations with climate change goals.

ADB is working to solidify its role as Asia and the Pacific's climate bank. It has established a dedicated NDC support platform—NDC Advance—through which it provides DMCs with technical assistance to help refine and enhance their NDC commitments, translate these NDCs into climate investment plans, and identify priority climate projects. NDC Advance also helps improve DMC access to external public and private climate financing, particularly supporting the use of innovative finance mechanisms; and develops methods and tools to measure, monitor, and report on progress made on the NDCs.[3]

Under NDC Advance, the ADB project team conducted high-level urban climate assessments at the national level and for selected cities in Armenia, Georgia, and Uzbekistan.[4] The results of these assessments were developed into climate risk profiles that aim to provide urban focal agencies, ADB project teams, and other development practitioners with a reference guide for incorporating climate resilience in urban planning and management, as well as support government investment decisions and policy making. The risk profiles are presented in this publication as country chapters with three main sections: (i) climate trends and risk diagnostics (national and city levels), (ii) options for mainstreaming climate resilience in urban planning, and (iii) infrastructure design considerations. The country chapters are followed by a guidance note on the limitations of the risk profiles and how they should be interpreted. Annexes describing the methodological approaches used are available on request.

ADB's holistic resilience framework[5] can be used as a foundational principle and approach for mainstreaming climate resilience in urban planning and development. In this framework,

---

[1] ADB. 2021. ADB Raises 2019–2030 Climate Finance Ambition to $100 Billion. News release. 13 October.

[2] ADB. 2018. *Strategy 2030: Achieving a Prosperous, Inclusive, Resilient, and Sustainable Asia and the Pacific.* Manila.

[3] ADB. 2022. *NDC Adva nce: Accelerating Climate Actions in Asia and the Pacific.* Manila.

[4] ADB. 2019. *Technical Assistance for Supporting the Implementation of ADB's Climate Change Operational Framework 2017–2030—Subproject 1: Supporting Ambitious Climate Action through Implementation of Developing Member Countries' Nationally Determined Contributions.* Manila.

[5] Further described in X. Lu. 2019. Building Resilient Infrastructure for the Future: Background Paper for the G20 Climate Sustainability Working Group. *ADB Sustainable Development Working Paper Series.* No. 61. Manila: ADB.

system resilience is identified as a product of ecosystem, infrastructure, financial, and social and institutional resilience. The risk profiles spotlighted in this publication draw on this holistic framework by emphasizing the integration of nature-based solutions, operation and maintenance (O&M) considerations, and capacity building and other institutional enhancement measures.

The risk profiles have contributed to the design and climate assessment of three ADB urban and water projects: two in Georgia, and one in Uzbekistan.[6] These projects are supporting nine of the 15 profiled localities, including Tbilisi, Batumi, Kutaisi, Mestia-Lentekhi, Northern Kakheti, and Zugdidi in Georgia; and Djizzak, Khiva, and Yangiyer in Uzbekistan. Another profiled locality, Armenia's capital city of Yerevan, is also being supported by the ongoing ADB-funded Sustainable Urban Development Investment Program. More information on the urban trends in Armenia, Georgia, and Uzbekistan is available in ADB's national urban assessment for each of the countries in focus.[7]

---

[6]   These new investments include the Sustainable Water Supply and Sanitation Sector Development Program and Livable Cities Investment Project in Georgia and the Integrated Urban Development Project in Uzbekistan.

[7]   Specifically (i) ADB. 2019. *Armenia's Transformative Urban Future: National Urban Assessment*. Manila; (ii) ADB. 2016. *Realizing the Urban Potential in Georgia: National Urban Assessment*. Manila; and (iii) ADB. 2021. *Harnessing Uzbekistan's Potential of Urbanization: National Urban Assessment*. Manila.

COUNTRY CHAPTERS

1. Armenia

1.1 Climate Trends and Risk Analyses: National Level

SUMMARY (2050)

Averages
- Increase in average yearly temperature predicted by all climate models
- Slight downward trend evident in projections of precipitation

Extremes
- Increases in maximum yearly temperature and number of days where a temperature of more than 35 degrees Celsius suggests increasing frequency and intensity of heat waves
- Increases in maximum 1-day precipitation events may lead to increased flood risk

Seasonality
- Increases in average temperatures for all months
- Shift predicted in seasonality of precipitation, with the months of June–September becoming drier

Spatial distribution
- Southwestern provinces most exposed to temperature increases and extreme heat events
- Western provinces likely to experience increases in precipitation and extreme rainfall events

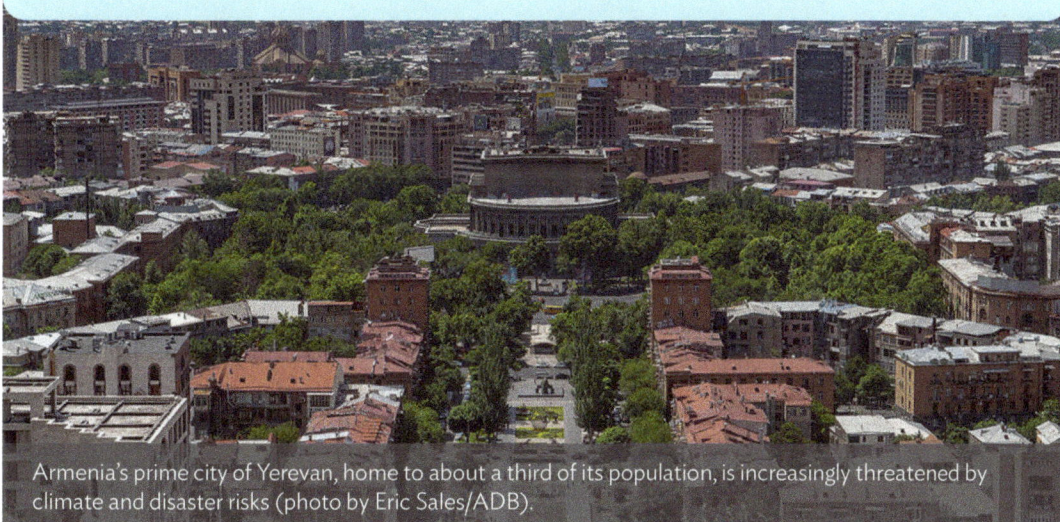

Armenia's prime city of Yerevan, home to about a third of its population, is increasingly threatened by climate and disaster risks (photo by Eric Sales/ADB).

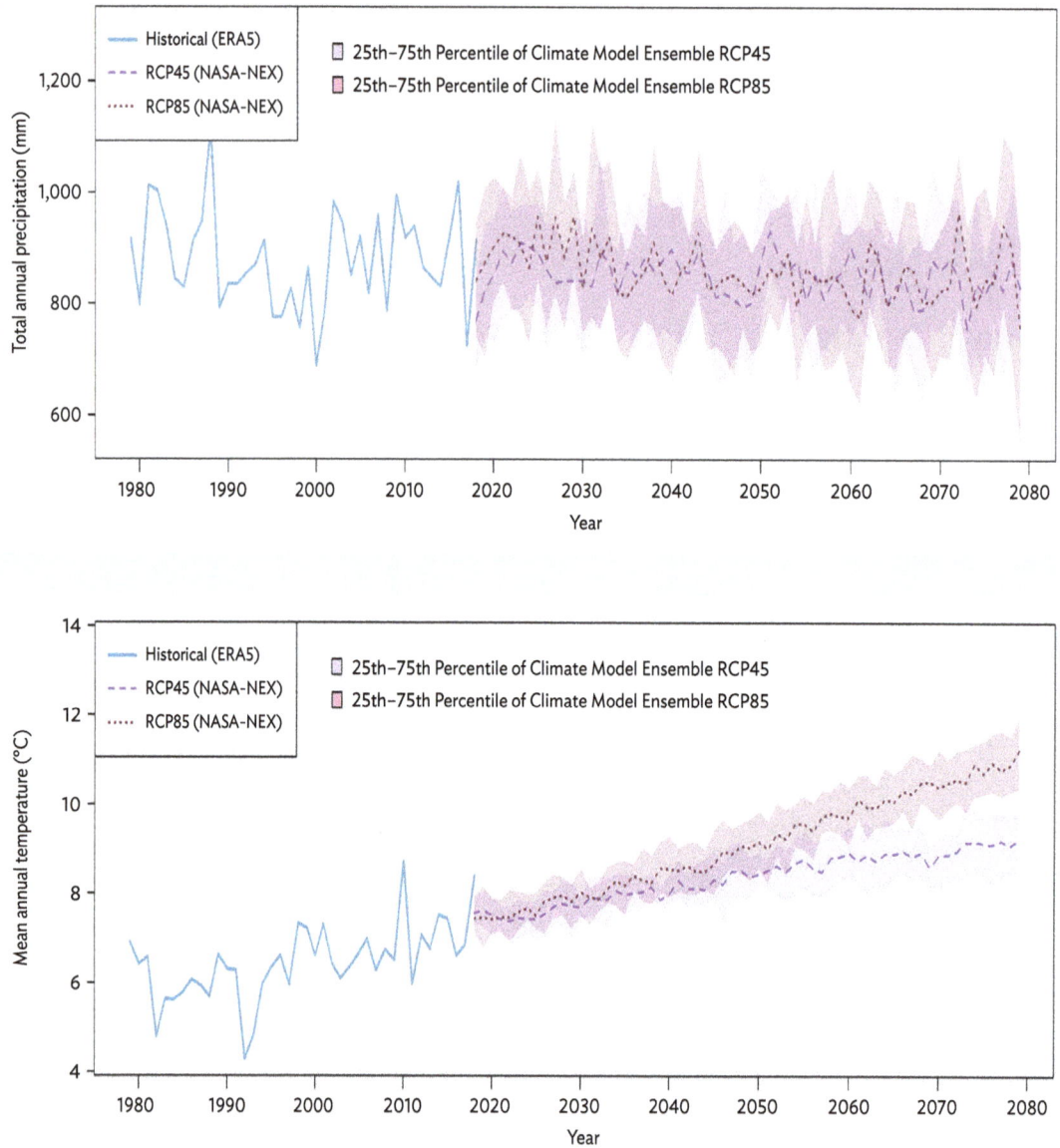

Figure 1.1: Past and Future Changes in Temperature and Precipitation under Medium and High Emissions Scenarios (Armenia)

mm = millimeter, NASA-NEX = NASA Earth Exchange, RCP = representative concentration pathway.

Notes: Shaded areas indicate the 25th and 75th percentiles of climate model ensemble predictions, reflecting the full spread of model predictions. ERA5 refers to the 5th generation atmospheric reanalysis of the global climate, covering 1950 to the present.

Source: Asian Development Bank project team and consultant experts, using data from ERA5 (historical) and NASA-NEX climate model projections (RCP45 and RCP85).

Figure 1.2: Per-Province Changes in Temperature and Precipitation under a Medium Emissions Scenario (Armenia)

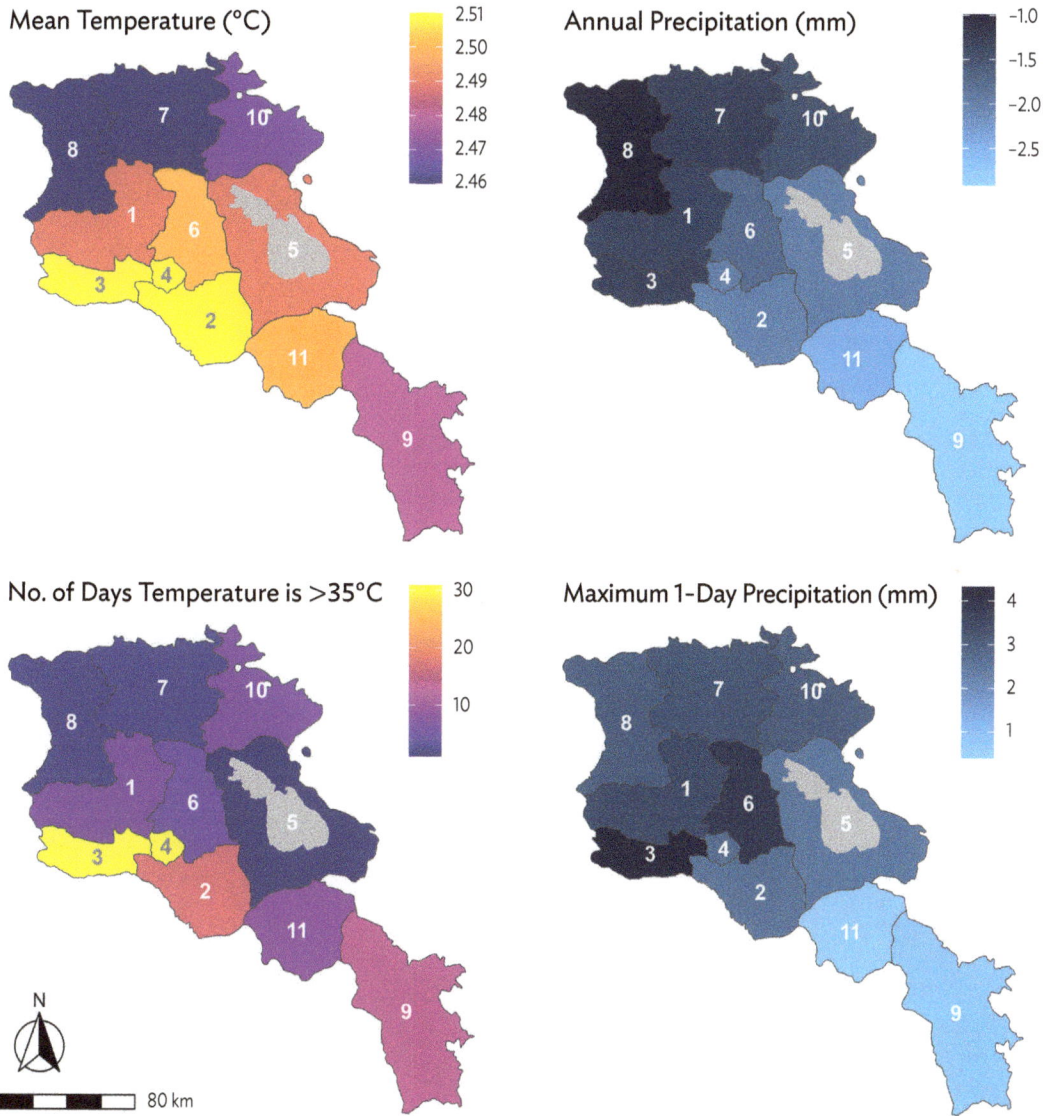

> = greater than, mm = millimeter, RCP = representative concentration pathway.

Notes: Spatial trends represent changes from the historical (1990) to the future (2050) RCP45 scenario.
ERA5 refers to the 5th generation atmospheric reanalysis of the global climate, covering 1950 to the present.

Source: Asian Development Bank project team and consultant experts, using data from ERA5 and NASA Earth Exchange.

Table 1.1: Summary of National-Level Changes in Future Climate under Medium and High Emissions Scenarios (Armenia)

Variable	Units [Δ units]	Historic	Δ RCP45 2030	Δ RCP45 2050	Δ RCP85 2030	Δ RCP85 2050
Average climate trends						
Mean Annual Temperature	°C [°C]	12.8	**1.4**	**2.2**	**1.5**	**2.9**
			[0.8, 1.9]	[1.5, 2.7]	[0.9, 2.1]	[2.1, 3.6]
Total Annual Precipitation	mm/year [%]	511	**0.1**	**(1.10)**	**0.6**	**(4.50)**
			[(11.3), 13.1]	[(14.5), 14.2]	[(13.4), 16.2]	[(18.3), 12.1]
Extreme temperature trends						
Maximum Annual Temperature	°C [°C]	32.6	**2**	**2.9**	**2.3**	**4**
			[1, 3]	[1.9, 4]	[1.2, 3.2]	[2.8, 5.3]
Minimum Annual Temperature	°C [°C]	(20.9)	**0.9**	**1.4**	**1.4**	**2.2**
			[(1.5), 3.4]	[(0.9), 4]	[(1.4), 3.9]	[(0.4), 4.6]
Extreme precipitation trends						
Maximum 1-Day Precipitation	mm/day [%]	27.8	**6.4**	**3.6**	**5.9**	**5.6**
			[(11.2), 23.4]	[(12.9), 23.8]	[(12.3), 24.5]	[(12.5), 27.8]
Drought Period Length	days [days]	27.8	**1.2**	**3.4**	**1.9**	**5.2**
			[(3.1), 6.5]	[(2), 11]	[(3.5), 10]	[(0.8), 13.4]

Δ = change, ( ) = negative, mm = millimeter, RCP = representative concentration pathway.

Notes: Numbers in brackets represent median values (25th percentile, 75th percentile) of climate model ensemble predictions.
        ERA5 refers to the 5th generation atmospheric reanalysis of the global climate, covering 1950 to the present.

Source: Asian Development Bank project team and consultant experts, using data from ERA5 (historical) and NASA Earth Exchange climate model projections (RCP45 and RCP85).

Shaded parks with resource-efficient cooling facilities, as seen in this Yerevan town square, are becoming increasingly important urban amenities, given the projected rising temperature for most parts of Armenia (photo by Eric Sales/ADB).

Figure 1.3: Seasonal Changes in Temperature and Precipitation, Historical and Future Time Horizons (Armenia)

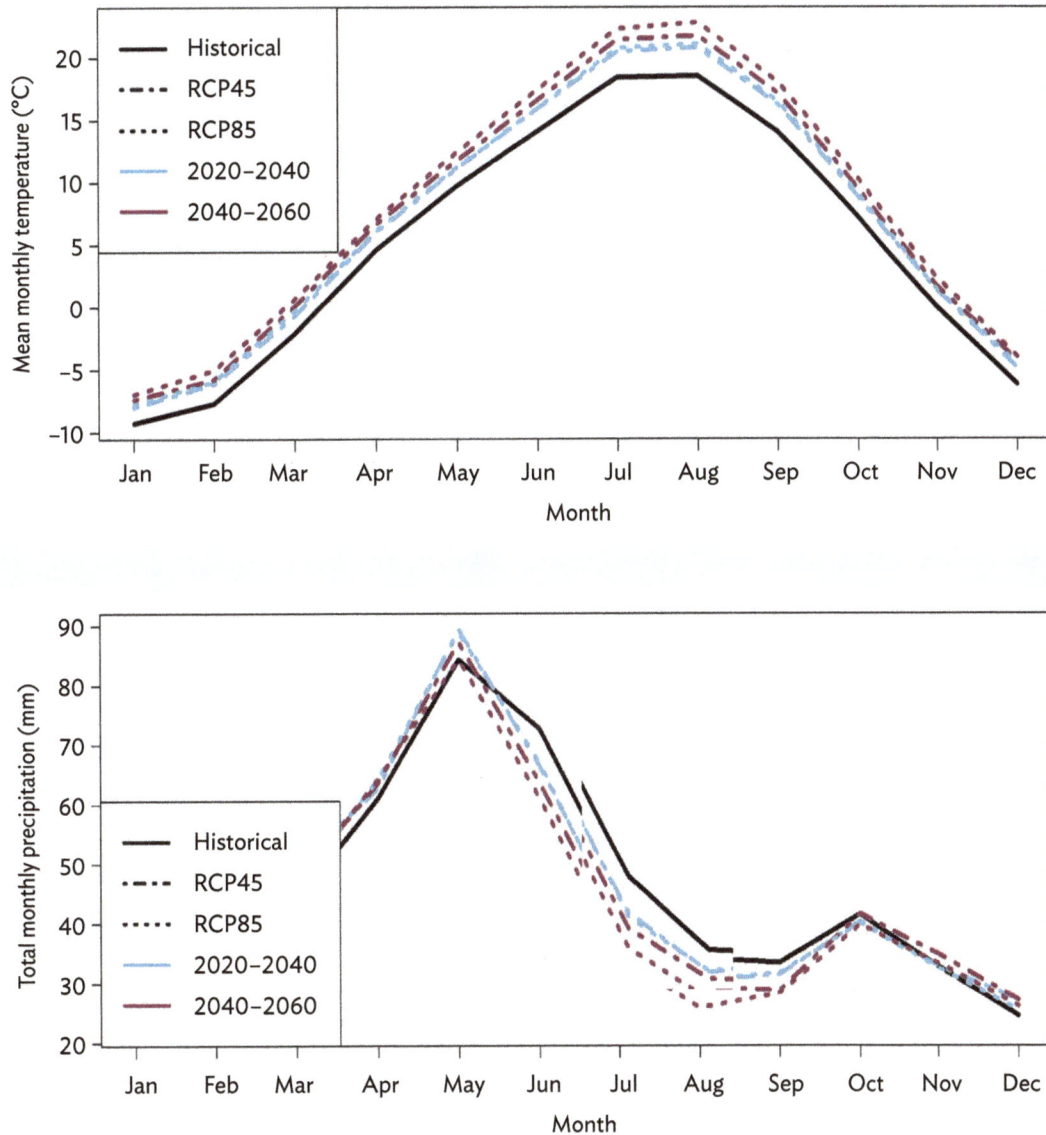

mm = millimeter, RCP = representative concentration pathway.

Notes: Historical data represent 1996–2015 reference period.
        ERA5 refers to the 5th generation atmospheric reanalysis of the global climate, covering 1950 to the present.

Source: Asian Development Bank project team and consultant experts, using data from ERA5 (historical) and NASA Earth Exchange climate model projections (RCP45 and RCP85).

1.2 Climate Trends and Risk Analyses: Gyumri (Shirak Province)

SUMMARY (2050)

City-scale risk
- Moderate risk of extreme heat events in the urban center
- Moderate riverine flood risk along road networks

National-scale hazards
- Unlikely to experience extreme water stress problems
- Extreme cold events are likely to affect area

Changes in climate
- Moderate increases in maximum yearly temperature will likely increase frequency and intensity of heat waves
- Small increases in maximum 1-day precipitation events may increase flood risk

Extreme precipitation
- The most severe precipitation events predicted by climate model ensemble are of moderate intensity

Figure 1.4: Current Risk Associated with Extreme Heat and Riverine Flooding (Gyumri)

Extreme Heat

Flooding

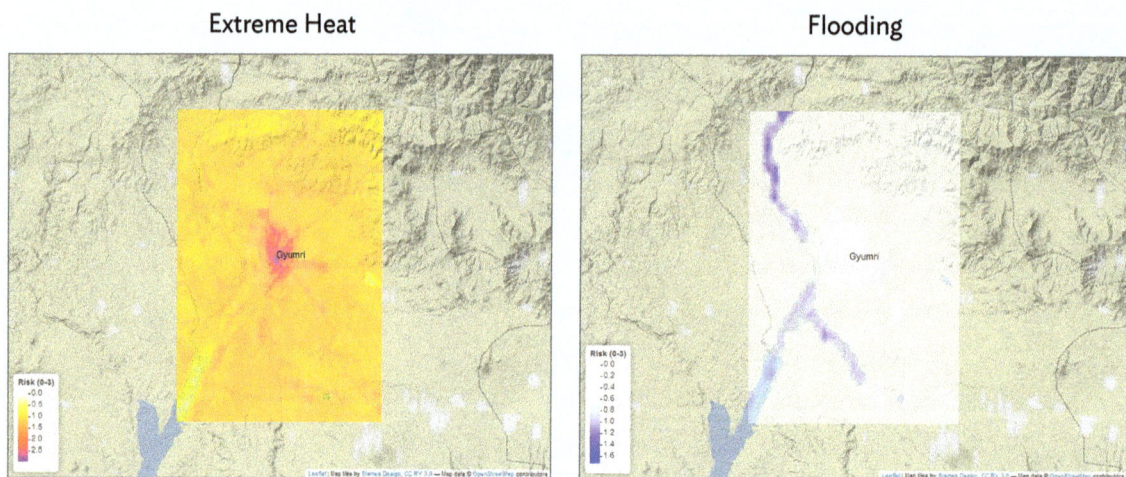

Note: 0 = no risk, 3 = high risk.

Source: Asian Development Bank project team and consultant experts, using data from the United Nations (population density and gross domestic product); OpenStreetMap (vulnerability of road networks, buildings, and points of interest); United Nations Office for Disaster Risk Reduction. 2015. *Global Assessment Report on Disaster Risk Reduction 2015*. Geneva (1 in 100-year flood hazard); and Google Earth Engine (heat anomaly signals).

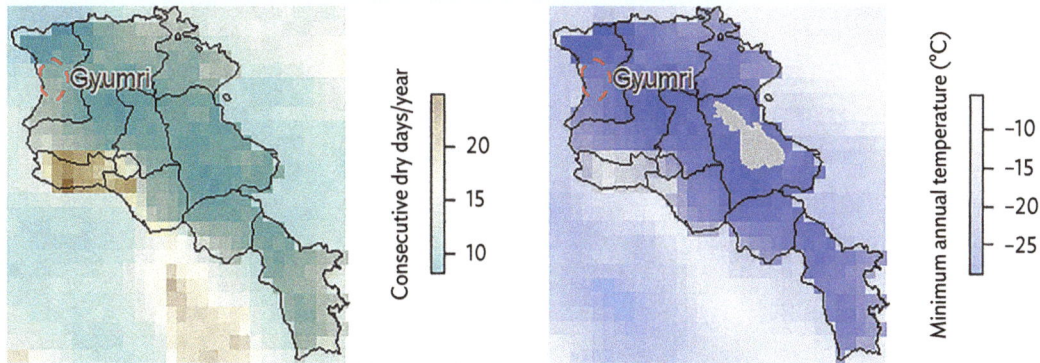

Figure 1.5: Current Hazards Associated with Water Shortage or Drought and Extreme Cold Events (Gyumri)

Notes: Map shows the spatial distribution of each hazard and the location of the urban area in this context.
ERA5 refers to the 5th generation atmospheric reanalysis of the global climate, covering 1950 to the present.
Source: Asian Development Bank project team and consultant experts, using data from ERA5 (drought and extreme low temperature).

Table 1.2: Changes in Future Climate under Medium and High Emissions Scenarios (Gyumri)

Variable	Units [Δ units]	Historic	Δ RCP45 2030	Δ RCP45 2050	Δ RCP85 2030	Δ RCP85 2050
Average climate trends						
Mean Annual Temperature	°C [°C]	11	1.3 [0.8, 1.9]	2.1 [1.5, 2.7]	1.5 [0.9, 2.1]	2.9 [2.2, 3.6]
Total Annual Precipitation	mm/year [%]	565.3	0.7 [(11.2), 13.7]	0.3 [(12.1), 15]	1.6 [(12.3), 17.8]	(3.2) [(17.8), 13.3]
Extreme temperature trends						
Maximum Annual Temperature	°C [°C]	31	1.8 [0.7, 3]	2.8 [1.7, 4]	2 [0.9, 3.3]	3.8 [2.6, 5.3]
Minimum Annual Temperature	°C [°C]	(24.9)	0.9 [(1.5), 3.3]	1.5 [(0.8), 4]	1.4 [(1.1), 3.9]	2.4 [(0.3,) 4.7]
Extreme precipitation trends						
Maximum 1-Day Precipitation	mm/day [%]	27.1	4.7 [(13.3), 26.1]	3.9 [(14.1), 26]	4.7 [(11.5), 29.1]	5.4 [(13.5), 29.3]
Drought Period Length	days [days]	24.3	1.4 [(2.7), 6.5]	2.4 [(2.4), 9.1]	1.4 [(3.8), 9.7]	3.7 [(1.6), 11.2]

Δ = change, ( ) = negative, mm = millimeter, RCP = representative concentration pathway.
Notes: Numbers in brackets represent median values (25th percentile, 75th percentile) of climate model ensemble predictions.
ERA5 refers to the 5th generation atmospheric reanalysis of the global climate, covering 1950 to the present.
Source: Asian Development Bank project team and consultant experts, using data from ERA5 (historical) and NASA Exchange climate model projections (RCP45 and RCP85).

Figure 1.6: Return Period Analysis of Extreme Precipitation Events (Gyumri)

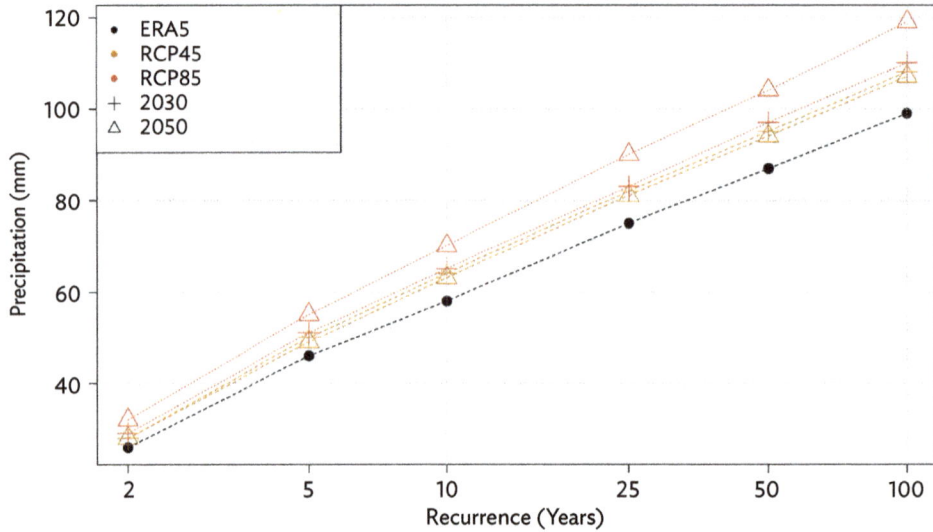

	Return Period					
	2 Years	5 Years	10 Years	25 Years	50 Years	100 Years
Historical daily maximum precipitation (mm)						
ERA5	26	46	58	75	87	99
Future (75th percentile of GCM distribution) (mm)						
RCP45 2030	28	50	64	82	95	108
RCP45 2050	28	49	63	81	94	107
RCP85 2030	29	51	65	83	97	110
RCP85 2050	32	55	70	90	104	119

Δ = change, GCM = global circulation model, mm = millimeter, RCP = representative concentration pathway.

Notes: The analysis represents changes in the yearly maximum 1-day precipitation (Rx1day) at various return periods, providing predictions of future frequencies of extreme precipitation events. It is based on the third quartile (75th percentile) of ensemble predictions and uses a Gumbel fitting approach to estimate the extreme events. The numbers can be used to inform the design of more climate-resilient urban infrastructure.

ERA5 refers to the 5th generation atmospheric reanalysis of the global climate, covering 1950 to the present.

Source: Asian Development Bank project team and consultant experts, using data from ERA5 (historical) and NASA Earth Exchange climate model projections (RCP45 and RCP85).

1.3   Climate Trends and Risk Analyses: Vanadzor (Lori Province)

SUMMARY (2050)

City-scale risk
- Moderate risk of extreme heat events across area, increased for urban area
- Moderate riverine flood risk along road networks

National-scale hazards
- Unlikely to experience extreme water stress problems
- Extreme cold events are likely to affect area

Changes in climate
- Large increases in maximum yearly temperature will likely increase frequency and intensity of heat waves
- Moderate increases in maximum 1-day precipitation events may increase flood risk

Extreme precipitation
- The most severe precipitation events predicted by climate model ensemble are of moderate intensity

Figure 1.7: Current Risk Associated with Extreme Heat and Riverine Flooding (Vanadzor)

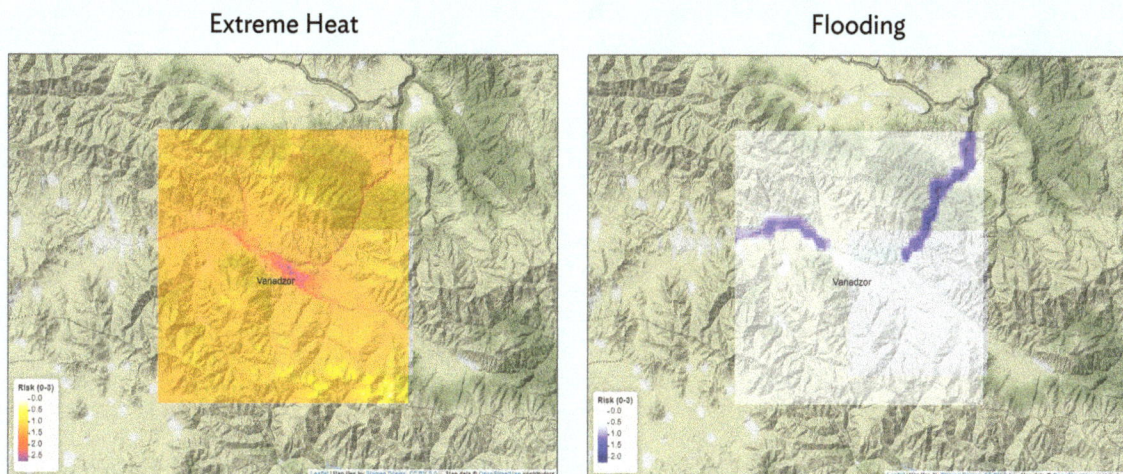

Note: 0 = no risk, 3 = high risk.

Source: Asian Development Bank project team and consultant experts, using data from the United Nations (population density and gross domestic product); OpenStreetMap (vulnerability of road networks, buildings, and points of interest); United Nations Office for Disaster Risk Reduction. 2015. *Global Assessment Report on Disaster Risk Reduction 2015.* Geneva (1 in 100-year flood hazard); and Google Earth Engine (heat anomaly signals).

Figure 1.8: Current Hazards Associated with Water Shortage or Drought and Extreme Cold Events (Vanadzor)

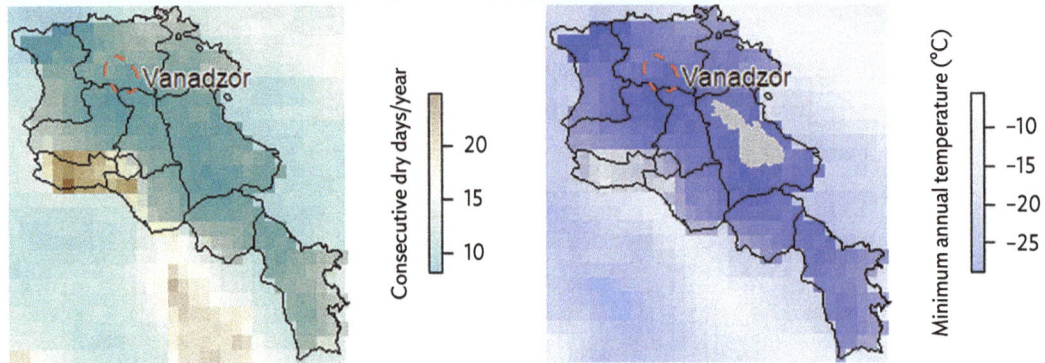

Notes: Map shows the spatial distribution of each hazard and the location of the urban area in this context.
ERA5 refers to the 5th generation atmospheric reanalysis of the global climate, covering 1950 to the present.

Source: Asian Development Bank project team and consultant experts, using data from ERA5 (drought and extreme low temperature).

Table 1.3: Changes in Future Climate under Medium and High Emissions Scenarios (Vanadzor)

Variable	Units [Δ units]	Historic	Δ RCP45 2030	Δ RCP45 2050	Δ RCP85 2030	Δ RCP85 2050
Average climate trends						
Mean Annual Temperature	°C [°C]	11.9	**1.4** [0.8, 1.9]	**2.1** [1.5, 2.7]	**1.5** [0.9, 2.1]	**2.9** [2.1, 3.6]
Total Annual Precipitation	mm/year [%]	597.5	**0.7** [(10.9), 14.6]	**0** [(12.8), 14.9]	**2.3** [(12), 18.1]	**(2.1)** [(18.1), 12.4]
Extreme temperature trends						
Maximum Annual Temperature	°C [°C]	31.5	**2** [0.9, 3.3]	**3.1** [1.8, 4.2]	**2.3** [1.1, 3.4]	**4** [2.8, 5.4]
Minimum Annual Temperature	°C [°C]	(22.2)	**0.8** [(1.7), 3.3]	**1.5** [(0.9), 3.9]	**1.2** [(1.2), 3.8]	**2.1** [(0.5), 4.6]
Extreme precipitation trends						
Maximum 1-Day Precipitation	mm/day [%]	29.1	**6.1** [(15.1), 32.3]	**5.1** [(15.5), 35.4]	**4.6** [(13.6), 33.9]	**5.7** [(13.9), 36.5]
Drought Period Length	days [days]	23.6	**1.4** [(3), 6.6]	**2.1** [(2.8), 9]	**1.4** [(3.6), 8.4]	**4.1** [(0.8), 11.4]

Δ = change, ( ) = negative, mm = millimeter, RCP = representative concentration pathway.

Notes: Numbers in brackets represent median values (25th percentile, 75th percentile) of climate model ensemble predictions.
ERA5 refers to the 5th generation atmospheric reanalysis of the global climate, covering 1950 to the present.

Source: Asian Development Bank project team and consultant experts, using data from ERA5 (historical) and NASA Earth Exchange climate model projections (RCP45 and RCP85).

Figure 1.9: Return Period Analysis of Extreme Precipitation Events (Vanadzor)

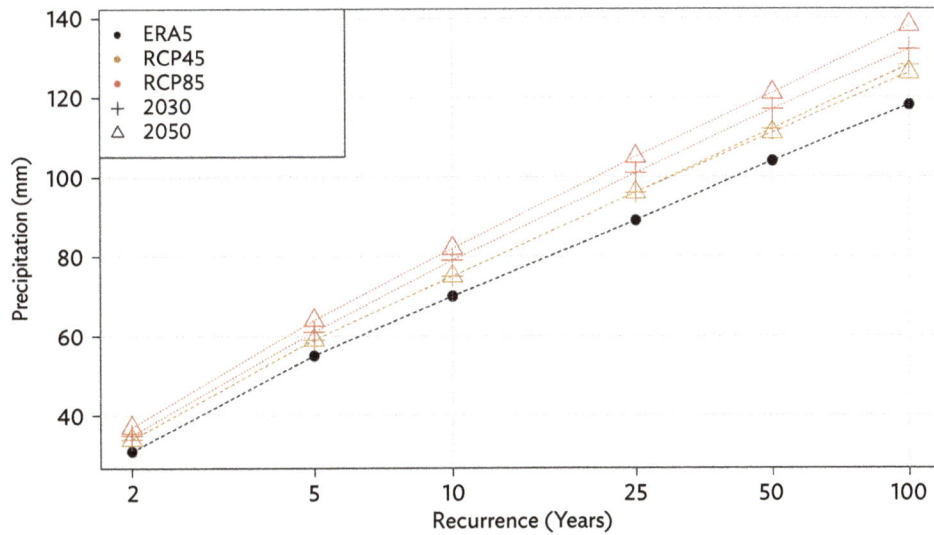

	Return Period					
	2 Years	5 Years	10 Years	25 Years	50 Years	100 Years
Historical daily maximum precipitation (mm)						
ERA5	31	55	70	89	104	118
Future (75th percentile of GCM distribution) (mm)						
RCP45 2030	34	59	75	96	112	128
RCP45 2050	34	59	75	96	111	126
RCP85 2030	35	61	79	101	117	132
RCP85 2050	37	64	82	105	121	138

Δ = change, GCM = global circulation model, mm = millimeter, RCP = representative concentration pathway.

Notes: The analysis represents changes in the yearly maximum 1-day precipitation (Rx1day) at various return periods, providing predictions of future frequencies of extreme precipitation events. It is based on the third quartile (75th percentile) of ensemble predictions and uses a Gumbel fitting approach to estimate the extreme events. The numbers can be used to inform the design of more climate-resilient urban infrastructure.

ERA5 refers to the 5th generation atmospheric reanalysis of the global climate, covering 1950 to the present.

Source: Asian Development Bank project team and consultant experts, using data from ERA5 (historical) and NASA Earth Exchange climate model projections (RCP45 and RCP85).

1.4 Climate Trends and Risk Analyses: Yerevan

SUMMARY (2050)

City-scale risk
- Moderate risk of extreme heat, concentrated in urban center
- Areas of moderate flood risk to south of urban center

National-scale hazards
- May be at some risk of experiencing water stress problems
- Area unlikely to be exposed to extreme cold events

Changes in climate
- Moderate increases in maximum yearly temperature increasing frequency and intensity of heat waves
- Small increases in maximum 1-day precipitation events may increase flood risk

Extreme precipitation
- The most severe precipitation events predicted by climate model ensemble are of low intensity

Figure 1.10: Current Risk Associated with Extreme Heat and Riverine Flooding (Yerevan)

Extreme Heat

Flooding

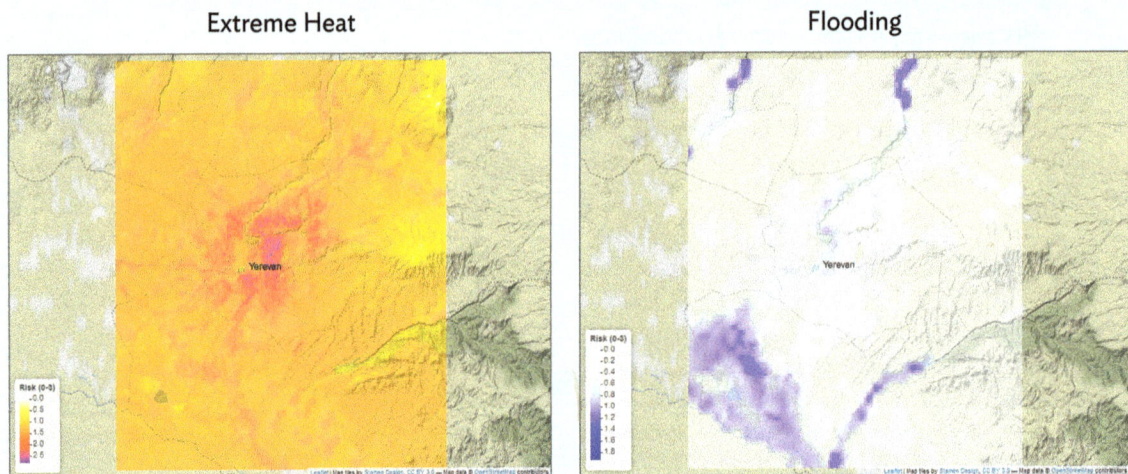

Note: 0 = no risk, 3 = high risk.

Source: Asian Development Bank project team and consultant experts, using data from the United Nations (population density and gross domestic product); OpenStreetMap (vulnerability of road networks, buildings, and points of interest); United Nations Office for Disaster Risk Reduction. 2015. *Global Assessment Report on Disaster Risk Reduction 2015*. Geneva (1 in 100-year flood hazard); and Google Earth Engine (heat anomaly signals).

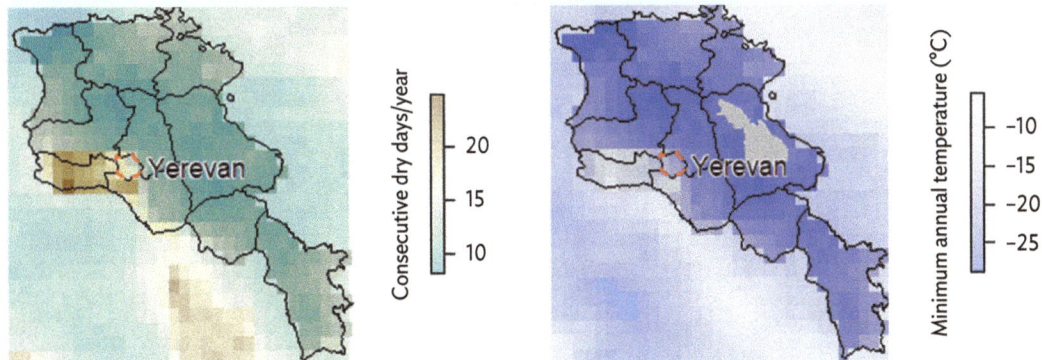

Figure 1.11: Current Hazards Associated with Water Shortage or Drought and Extreme Cold Events (Yerevan)

Notes: Map shows the spatial distribution of each hazard and the location of the urban area in this context.
ERA5 refers to the 5th generation atmospheric reanalysis of the global climate, covering 1950 to the present.

Source: Asian Development Bank project team and consultant experts, using data from ERA5 (drought and extreme low temperature).

Table 1.4: Changes in Future Climate under Medium and High Emissions Scenarios (Yerevan)

Variable	Units [Δ units]	Historic	Δ RCP45 2030	Δ RCP45 2050	Δ RCP85 2030	Δ RCP85 2050
Average climate trends						
Mean Annual Temperature	°C [°C]	17.5	1.3 [0.8, 1.9]	2.2 [1.5, 2.7]	1.5 [0.9, 2.2]	2.9 [2.2, 3.6]
Total Annual Precipitation	mm/year [%]	371.5	1.7 [(11.6), 14.6]	(0.5) [(14.9), 15.7]	2.1 [(12.9), 18.9]	(2.6) [(20.2), 14.4]
Extreme temperature trends						
Maximum Annual Temperature	°C [°C]	37.4	1.9 [0.8, 3.1]	2.9 [1.8, 4]	2.2 [1, 3.2]	3.9 [2.5, 5.4]
Minimum Annual Temperature	°C [°C]	(16.9)	0.8 [(1.5), 3.5]	1.5 [(1.1), 4.1]	1.2 [(1.4), 3.8]	2.2 [(0.4), 4.8]
Extreme precipitation trends						
Maximum 1-Day Precipitation	mm/day [%]	19.3	1.8 [(16.7), 34.1]	4.9 [(20.3), 33.4]	4.6 [(17.1), 35.4]	5.9 [(15.7), 37.7]
Drought Period Length	days [days]	30.8	0.2 [(4.8), 9.2]	4.2 [(3.8), 12.8]	1.2 [(4.8), 11.2]	5.2 [(2.8), 16.2]

Δ = change, ( ) = negative, mm = millimeter, RCP = representative concentration pathway.

Notes: Numbers in brackets represent median values (25th percentile, 75th percentile) of climate model ensemble predictions.
ERA5 refers to the 5th generation atmospheric reanalysis of the global climate, covering 1950 to the present.

Source: Asian Development Bank project team and consultant experts, using data from ERA5 (historical) and NASA Earth Exchange climate model projections (RCP45 and RCP85).

Figure 1.12: Return Period Analysis of Extreme Precipitation Events (Yerevan)

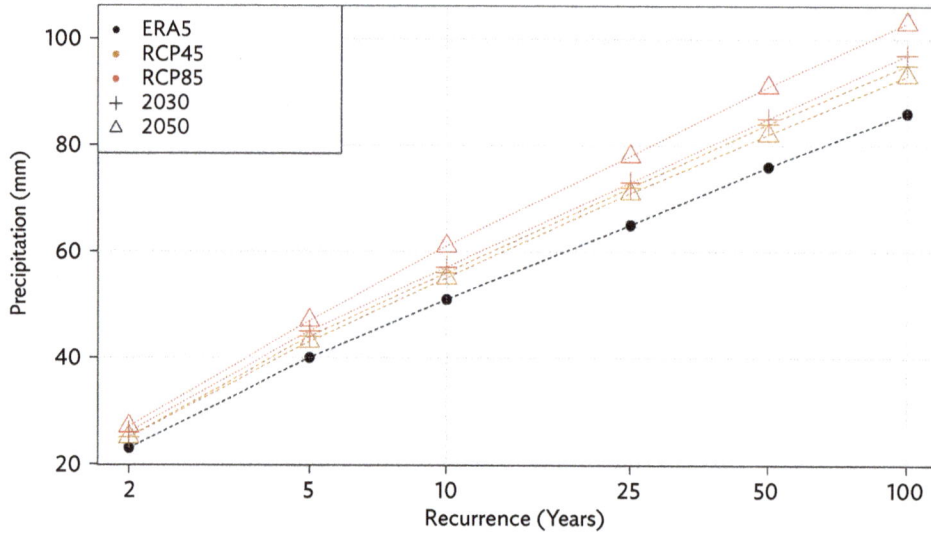

	Return Period					
	2 Years	5 Years	10 Years	25 Years	50 Years	100 Years
Historical daily maximum precipitation (mm)						
ERA5	23	40	51	65	76	86
Future (75th percentile of GCM distribution) (mm)						
RCP45 2030	25	44	56	72	84	95
RCP45 2050	25	43	55	71	82	93
RCP85 2030	26	45	57	73	85	97
RCP85 2050	27	47	61	78	91	103

Δ = change, GCM = global circulation model, mm = millimeter, RCP = representative concentration pathway.

Notes: The analysis represents changes in the yearly maximum 1-day precipitation (Rx1day) at various return periods, providing predictions of future frequencies of extreme precipitation events. It is based on the third quartile (75th percentile) of ensemble predictions and uses a Gumbel fitting approach to estimate the extreme events. The numbers can be used to inform the design of more climate-resilient urban infrastructure.

ERA5 refers to the 5th generation atmospheric reanalysis of the global climate, covering 1950 to the present.

Source: Asian Development Bank project team and consultant experts, using data from ERA5 (historical) and NASA Earth Exchange climate model projections (RCP45 and RCP85).

1.5 Options for Mainstreaming Climate Change in Urban Planning

Key Considerations in Selected Subsectors

Adaptation starts at the planning stage. Taking climate change risks into account in both land-use planning and siting of infrastructure is of paramount importance, as is answering questions such as "Which infrastructure projects are needed to enhance urban climate resilience?" And "Is this project appropriate within the urban risk context?"

Focusing on key subsectors that may be affected by climate change and correspond to priority areas of ADB investment, Table 1.5 provides some specific measures that may be considered in the national-level urban planning process. Although relevant, health and energy are beyond the scope of this risk profile.

Table 1.5: Planning Considerations for Selected Urban Subsectors

Projected Climate Change	Relevance to Area (Low/Medium/High)[a]	Potential Impacts on Infrastructure	Possible Planning Considerations and/or Actions
Transport Infrastructure			
Small to moderate increases in precipitation intensity, maximum 1-day precipitation events	High Moderate precipitation in country, which is likely an issue along large river channels. The mountainous terrain makes the country vulnerable to flash flooding, pluvial flooding, and landslides.	Increased precipitation potentially leading to increased damage to roads and transport infrastructure because of floods, mudslides, landslides, and avalanches	• Take into account the flooding risks in decisions regarding the siting of roads and rails and related infrastructure • Incorporate blue spaces and green spaces in planning to cope with excess water[b] • Encourage mixed-use, vertical, and compact development as opposed to urban sprawl to reduce dependence on car-centric lifestyles
Moderate increase in maximum temperatures and frequency of heat waves	Medium The country does not experience extreme heat regularly, although urban centers are at risk of the urban heat island effect.	Intense heat waves and increased temperatures potentially affecting transport infrastructure and requiring more frequent repairs, as well as affecting users	Encourage the use of nature-based solutions such as tree planting, creation of urban water bodies, and green roofs to reduce the urban heat island effect[c]
Moderate increase in minimum yearly temperatures, considerable decrease in frost days	Medium This is most likely to occur in higher elevation areas throughout the country.	Increases in minimum temperatures potentially leading to a decrease in frost- and ice-related damage to infrastructure	No adaptation needed to address climate change risks, possibly a gain from climate change to be realized

continued on next page

Table 1.5 *continued*

Projected Climate Change	Relevance to Area (Low/Medium/High)[a]	Potential Impacts on Infrastructure	Possible Planning Considerations and/or Actions
Buildings			
Small to moderate increases in precipitation intensity, maximum 1-day precipitation events	**High** Moderate precipitation, which is likely an issue along large river channels. The mountainous nature of the country is likely to lead to problems of flash flooding, pluvial flooding, and landslides.	Increased precipitation potentially leading to increased damage to buildings because of floods, mudslides, landslides, and avalanches	• Climate informed land-use planning (e.g., siting of buildings) • Climate-resilient building codes • Upgrading of existing surface water management and drainage infrastructure for increased intensity precipitation events • Incorporation of SUDS features in the planning process • Early warning systems[d]
Moderate increase in maximum temperatures and frequency of heat waves	**Medium** The country does not experience extreme heat regularly, although this may be an issue in large urban centers.	Intense heat waves and increased temperatures potentially affecting buildings and users	• Building codes to improve temperature regulation in buildings and encourage the use of heat-resistant materials • Green-blue infrastructure such as urban green space, water features, green roofs, and shading trees
Moderate increase in minimum yearly temperatures, considerable decrease in frost days	**Medium** This is most likely to occur in higher-elevation areas throughout the country.	Increases in minimum temperatures potentially leading to a decrease in frost- and ice-related damage to buildings	No adaptation needed to address climate change risks, possibly a gain from climate change to be realized
Sanitation, Sewerage, and Water Supply			
Moderate increases in precipitation intensity, maximum 1-day precipitation events	**High** This is likely an issue in areas with extreme topography, and expansive urban areas.	Increased extreme precipitation events may exceed urban water cycle capacity	• Enhance land-use planning, focusing on increasing the percentage of permeable and semipermeable green space and creating water storage and retention in urban areas[e] • Upgrade capacity of sewerage networks • Shift from combined sewerage and drainage networks to separate systems • Incorporate SUDSs in drainage planning • Create climate-resilient drainage and wastewater management plans
Small increase in drought length, decrease or small increase in total precipitation	**Medium** The country experiences some water stress.	Increased intensity of droughts may cause water shortages	• Measures to increase water efficiency (loss reduction) in infrastructure • Demand for management measures[f] • Diversification of water supply, water recycling, and use of alternative water resources[g] • Creation of drought management and early warning strategies

continued on next page

Table 1.5 *continued*

Projected Climate Change	Relevance to Area (Low/Medium/High)[a]	Potential Impacts on Infrastructure	Possible Planning Considerations and/or Actions
Solid Waste			
Moderate increase in maximum annual temperatures	Medium This is most likely to occur in higher elevation areas throughout the country where the climate may become milder.	Increased temperature may require an improvement of the waste management system to cope with potentially increased risks of pathogenic germs to health	• Awareness raising and waste minimization campaigns around the 3Rs (reduce, reuse, and recycle) • Upgrading of landfill sites to avoid mobilization of pollutants and reduce methane emissions

SUDS = sustainable urban drainage system.

[a] Relevance ratings are determined by expert judgment based on relevant datasets presented in the climate risk profiles.

[b] Armenia's first nationally determined contribution, updated in April 2021, emphasizes ecosystem-based approaches. Government of Armenia. 2021. *Nationally Determined Contribution 2021–2030 of the Republic of Armenia to the Paris Agreement.* Yerevan.

[c] More guidance may be obtained from J. Matthews and E. O. Dela Cruz. 2022. *Integrating Nature-Based Solutions for Climate Change Adaptation and Disaster Risk Management: A Practitioner's Guide.* Manila: ADB.

[d] The country's fourth national communication specifically mentions the need for early warning systems to mitigate climate risks. Government of Armenia. 2020. *Armenia's Fourth National Communication on Climate Change under the United Nations Framework Convention on Climate Change.* Yerevan.

[e] See the "sponge city" concept piloted in several cities in the People's Republic of China with support from ADB. ADB. 2017. Piloting "Sponge Cities" in the People's Republic of China. Project result/case study. 13 January.

[f] This includes a variety of measures such as tariffs, pricing, user controls, awareness raising, and smart network monitoring.

[g] There are technologies that can use brackish water or wastewater as inputs and produce a combination of food (aquaculture products, vegetables, animal feed) and clean water. Applicability for Armenia would need to be assessed. The advantage of such technology is that it involves an ecosystem-based approach in line with Armenia's nationally determined contribution.

Source: Asian Development Bank project team.

Considerations on Enabling Environment, Local Government Planning, and Operation and Maintenance

Early action on other general considerations relating to planning and O&M can further accelerate urban climate resiliency building in Armenia. Some of these considerations are outlined below.

Building an enabling environment for climate-resilient planning

The central government can consider the following measures:

- Ensure that local governments and stakeholders are equipped with adequate data, information, and skills that will help them respond to the impacts of climate change. This could be in the form of data portals and knowledge-sharing workshops.

- Ensure that cities coping with climate change have sufficient access to finance, e.g., through applications by the central government to international climate financing facilities such as the Green Climate Fund.

- Ensure that individuals and communities affected by climate change-related hazards can recover and rebuild as quickly as possible via access to insurance and national government support programs.

- Develop building codes and standards for infrastructure that adequately take account of changes in climate, such as new flood return periods.

- Introduce and institutionalize risk-based land use and open space planning. Introduce blue-green resilience networks and nature-based solutions as a first step in spatial planning.
- Initiate and sustain benchmarking and monitoring of efforts across cities and local government jurisdictions, facilitating knowledge transfer between these parties.

Local government planning

Local governments may wish to consider the following measures:

- Consistently take account of how expected climate change interacts with the cities' development visions and how expected climate change may impact the relative viability of investments. This is especially relevant with regard to the performance of built assets over their respective project life cycles.
- Develop hazard maps to guide urban development, e.g., to integrate flood risks into urban spatial planning. This requires local-scale, higher-resolution modeling to better map the influence on hazards of a full envelope of likely changes in climate.
- Ensure that individuals and communities at risk to climate-related hazards are aware of the risks they are exposed to and how these may change in the future. This could be achieved via community outreach and digital applications.
- Climate hazard information should be factored into the design and implementation of development regulation instruments, such as zoning, land subdivision, and building codes. This will help reduce climate change vulnerability and avoid the expansion of development to high-risk areas.
- Adopt, implement, and enforce building codes and infrastructure standards that consider changes in climate, such as new flood return periods.
- Promote the development of early warning systems and climate change-related disaster response strategies (often as part of a more comprehensive disaster response strategy).
- Initiate community education programs for disaster preparedness. These should focus on preparing communities for situations in which authorities and emergency services are unable to access affected areas to provide critical assistance in the aftermath of a disaster.
- Undertake institutional strengthening for climate action through reform of responsibilities and the creation of a high-level climate change office under the governor and mayor and cross-departmental working groups.

Operation and maintenance

Adequate O&M is as important as up-front capital investments to enhance resilience to climate risk. Some key considerations relating to O&M are in the following list:

- Ensure that risk-informed O&M is considered from the earliest stages of planning and design for new infrastructure projects.
- Update existing O&M plans to reflect changes in precipitation and temperature, which may necessitate more frequent maintenance or changes in operational practices.
- Create backup emergency infrastructure in case of failure in key infrastructure, e.g., the maintenance of emergency generators in case of power failure.

- Ensure regular inspection and maintenance of infrastructure relating to hazard protection, e.g., flood protection structures.

- Implement smart monitoring strategies and the Internet of Things, which can collect, centralize, and review data relating to hydrometeorology and key infrastructure.

- Implement risk-informed preventive maintenance, which may be a highly feasible and cost-effective approach for ensuring overall network resilience.

- Prioritize O&M of telecommunication networks, which play a critical role in disaster response efforts.

1.6 Infrastructure Design Considerations

Table 1.6 provides some key considerations for the design and/or upgrading of urban infrastructure assets to enhance climate resilience based on expert judgment of climate model ensemble outputs, including possible adaptation measures. As with Table 1.5, this table focuses on key urban subsectors that may be affected by climate change and correspond to the priority areas of ADB investment. Health and energy, although also relevant, are beyond the scope of this profile.

Table 1.6: Design Considerations for Urban Infrastructure in Selected Cities

Projected Climate Change	Relevance to Area (Low/Medium/High)			Potential Impacts on Infrastructure	Possible Adaptation Measures
	Gyumri	Vanadzor	Yerevan	Gyumri, Vanadzor, Yerevan	
Transport Infrastructure					
Small increases in precipitation intensity, maximum 1-day precipitation events	Medium Riverine flood risk along road networks and west of urban center	Medium Riverine flood risk along road networks, some risk of landslides and pluvial flooding	Medium Some riverine flood risk to the southwest of city center	Increased precipitation potentially leading to increased damage to roads and transport infrastructure because of floods, mudslides, landslides, and avalanches	• Enhance drainage • Reinforce vulnerable structures • Utilize permeable roads and pavements • Increase the height and setback of flood defenses and dikes
Moderate increase in maximum temperatures and frequency of heat waves	Medium Problematic in urban centers, along road networks		High Risk concentrated in large urban centers	Intense heat waves and increased temperatures potentially affecting transport infrastructure and requiring more frequent repairs, as well as affecting users	• Use road construction materials that are more resistant to heat[a] • Use road construction materials with self-healing properties[b] • Plant trees along roadsides • Enhance ventilation and cooling for public transport systems

continued on next page

Table 1.6 *continued*

Projected Climate Change	Relevance to Area (Low/Medium/High)			Potential Impacts on Infrastructure	Possible Adaptation Measures
	Gyumri	Vanadzor	Yerevan	Gyumri, Vanadzor, Yerevan	
Moderate increase in minimum yearly temperatures, considerable decrease in frost days	**Medium** Likely more common in urban centers		**Medium** Extreme low temperatures will be less frequent, even less so in warm city centers	Increases in minimum temperatures potentially leading to a decrease in frost- and ice-related damage to infrastructure	No adaptation needed to address climate change risks, possibly a gain from climate change to be realized
Buildings					
Small increases in precipitation intensity, maximum 1-day precipitation events	**Medium** Riverine flood risk to the west of urban centers	**Medium** Limited riverine flood risk in urban centers, some risk of landslides and pluvial flooding	**High** High riverine flood risk in urban center	Increased precipitation potentially leading to increased damage to buildings because of floods, mudslides, landslides, and avalanches	• Enhanced drainage infrastructure to cope with increased intensity precipitation events • SUDSs, e.g., retention basins, bioswales • Daylighting of streams and river and/or floodplain restoration • Protective infrastructure such as flood barriers, slope stabilization measures, and dams • Bracing technologies against strong winds
Moderate increase in maximum temperatures and frequency of heat waves	**Medium** Most pertinent in urban centers		**High** Risk concentrated in large urban centers	Intense heat waves and increased temperatures potentially affecting buildings and users	• White roofs • Green roofs and shading trees • Airtight sealing and double-glazing of glass windows and doors • Increased thermal mass of buildings • Use of heat-reflective materials to minimize solar heat gain • Provision of ventilation • Efficient cooling[c]
Moderate increase in minimum yearly temperatures, considerable decrease in frost days	**Medium** Likely more common in urban centers		**Medium** Extreme low temperatures will be less frequent, even less so in warm city centers	Increases in minimum temperatures potentially leading to a decrease in frost- and ice-related damage to buildings	No adaptation needed to address climate change risks, possibly a climate change gain to be realized

continued on next page

Table 1.6 *continued*

Projected Climate Change	Relevance to Area (Low/Medium/High)			Potential Impacts on Infrastructure	Possible Adaptation Measures
	Gyumri	Vanadzor	Yerevan	Gyumri, Vanadzor, Yerevan	
Sanitation, Sewerage, and Water Supply					
Small increases in precipitation intensity, maximum 1-day precipitation events	Medium		Low May be complicated by complexities because of size of city	Increased extreme precipitation events may exceed urban water cycle capacity	• Upgrade drainage and sewerage assets to increase capacity for high-intensity precipitation events • Install SUDSs, e.g., bioswales, retention basins • Consider separating stormwater and wastewater • Install treatment wetlands to support wastewater treatment infrastructure
Small increase in drought length, increase in total precipitation	Low Limited drought problems in area		Medium Low total precipitation in area, may be aggravated by complexities because of size of city	Potentially increased intensity of droughts may cause water shortages	• Diversification of water sources: groundwater and surface water • Reuse and recycling of water • Rainwater harvesting • Reuse of wastewater for agricultural irrigation and industrial purposes
Solid Waste Management					
Moderate increase in maximum temperatures	Medium May be problematic in urban centers			Increased temperature may require an improvement of the waste management system to cope with potentially increased risks of pathogenic germs to health	• Enhanced waste collection, storage, and processing • Combination of recycling and reuse, anaerobic digestion, and incineration[d]

SUDS = sustainable urban drainage system.

[a] Examples include warm mix asphalt and engineered cementitious composites.

[b] Materials with self-healing properties are materials that automatically fill cracks without human intervention. Different materials (including concretes based on pozzolanic materials, concretes based on cements with added bacteria, and concrete with special coatings) can exhibit this behavior and may be used for road and bridge construction.

[c] Through the use of (i) efficient air conditioners with low global warming potential refrigerants, efficient chillers, and trigeneration technologies; and (ii) information technology to support energy efficiency in buildings using existing assets. Solution (ii) can be a low-cost option with a short payback period. It could also be considered a mitigation strategy as well as an adaptation measure. In specific locations, heat pumps using river water as a source of cooling can be a feasible option.

[d] Effective, commercially viable technologies exist for anaerobic digestion of waste and incineration for the generation of zero-emission power. Promotion of such technologies is in line with Armenia's first nationally determined contribution and could also be considered a mitigation strategy as well as an adaptation measure.

Source: Asian Development Bank project team.

2. Georgia

2.1 Climate Trends and Risk Analyses: National Level

SUMMARY (2050)

Averages
- Increase in average yearly temperature predicted by all climate models
- No clear signal in predictions for precipitation changes at the national level

Extremes
- Increases in maximum yearly temperature and number of days where a temperature of more than 35 degrees Celsius suggests increasing frequency and intensity of heat waves
- Increases in maximum 1-day precipitation events may increase flood risk

Seasonality
- Increases in average temperatures for all months
- Shift predicted in seasonality of precipitation, with earlier onset of rainy months, more extreme dry periods in July–September

Spatial distribution
- Southeastern provinces most exposed to temperature increases and extreme heat events
- Western provinces likely to experience increases in precipitation and extreme rainfall events

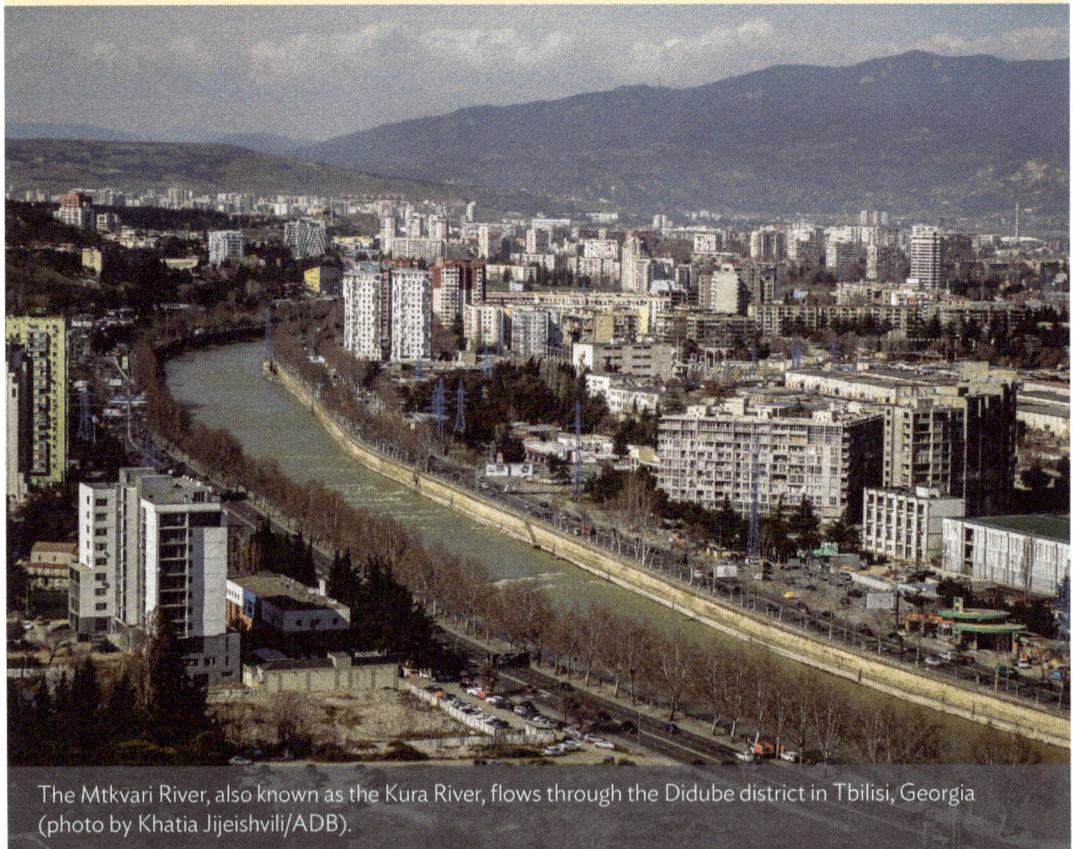

The Mtkvari River, also known as the Kura River, flows through the Didube district in Tbilisi, Georgia (photo by Khatia Jijeishvili/ADB).

Figure 2.1: Past and Future Changes in Temperature and Precipitation under Medium and High Emissions Scenarios (Georgia)

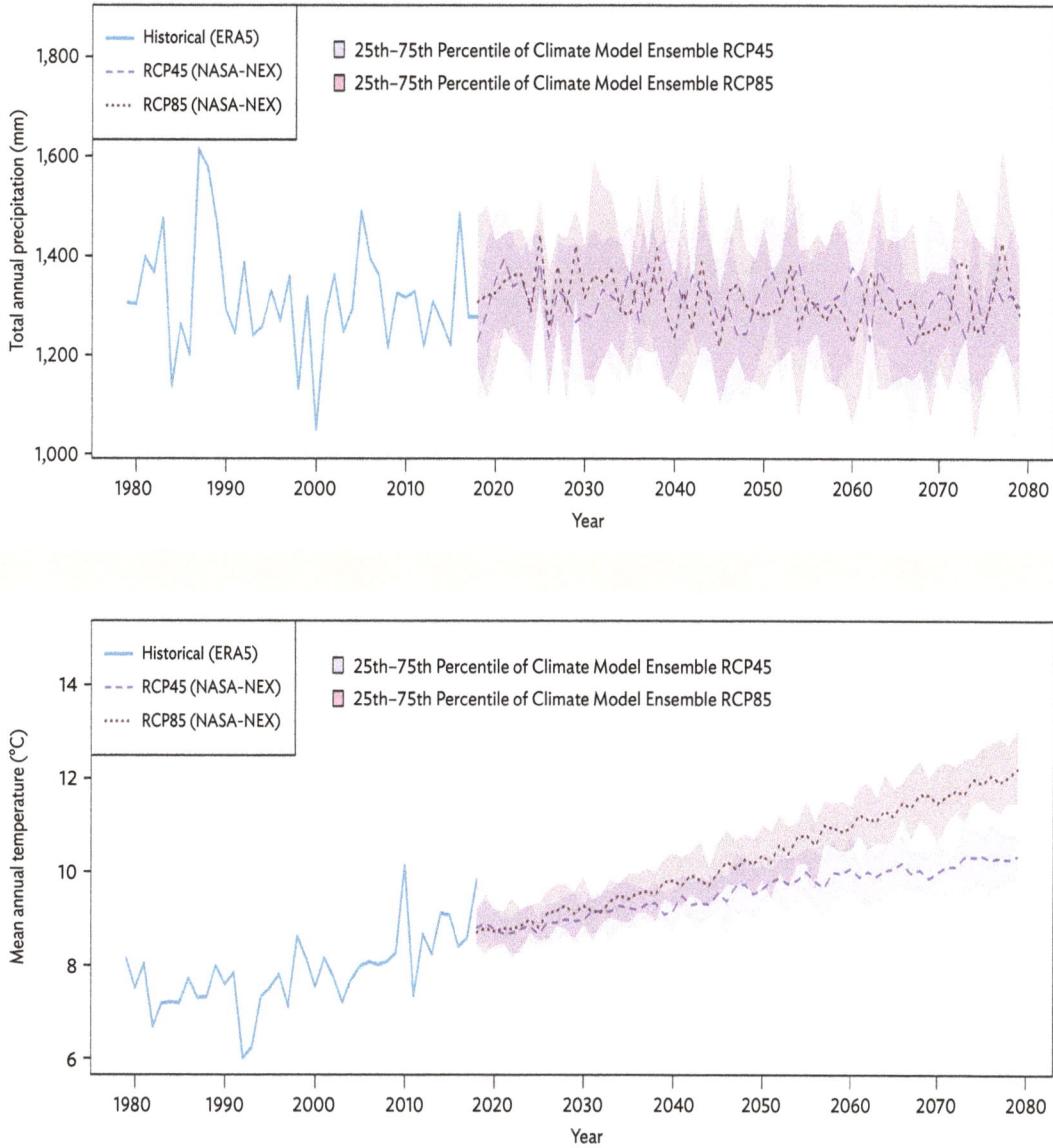

mm = millimeter, NASA-NEX = NASA Earth Exchange, RCP = representative concentration pathway.

Notes: Shaded areas indicate the 25th and 75th percentiles of climate model ensemble predictions, reflecting the full spread of model predictions. ERA5 refers to the 5th generation atmospheric reanalysis of the global climate, covering 1950 to the present.

Source: Asian Development Bank project team and consultant experts, using data from ERA5 (historical) and NASA-NEX climate model projections (RCP45 and RCP85).

Figure 2.2: Per-Province Changes in Temperature and Precipitation under a Medium Emissions Scenario (Georgia)

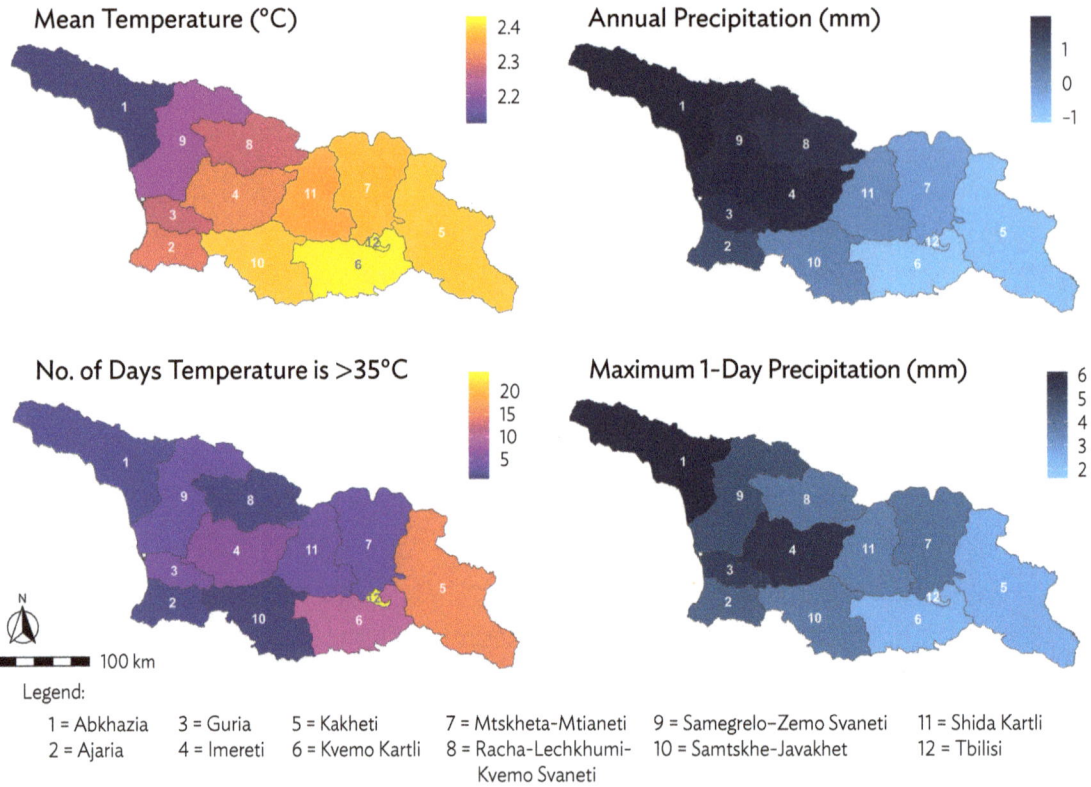

Mean Temperature (°C)

Annual Precipitation (mm)

No. of Days Temperature is >35°C

Maximum 1-Day Precipitation (mm)

100 km

Legend:
| 1 = Abkhazia | 3 = Guria | 5 = Kakheti | 7 = Mtskheta-Mtianeti | 9 = Samegrelo–Zemo Svaneti | 11 = Shida Kartli |
| 2 = Ajaria | 4 = Imereti | 6 = Kvemo Kartli | 8 = Racha-Lechkhumi-Kvemo Svaneti | 10 = Samtskhe-Javakhet | 12 = Tbilisi |

> = greater than, mm = millimeter, RCP = representative concentration pathway.

Notes: Spatial trends represent changes from the historical (1990) to the future (2050) RCP45 scenario.
ERA5 refers to the 5th generation atmospheric reanalysis of the global climate, covering 1950 to the present.

Source: Asian Development Bank project team and consultant experts, using data from ERA5 and NASA Earth Exchange.

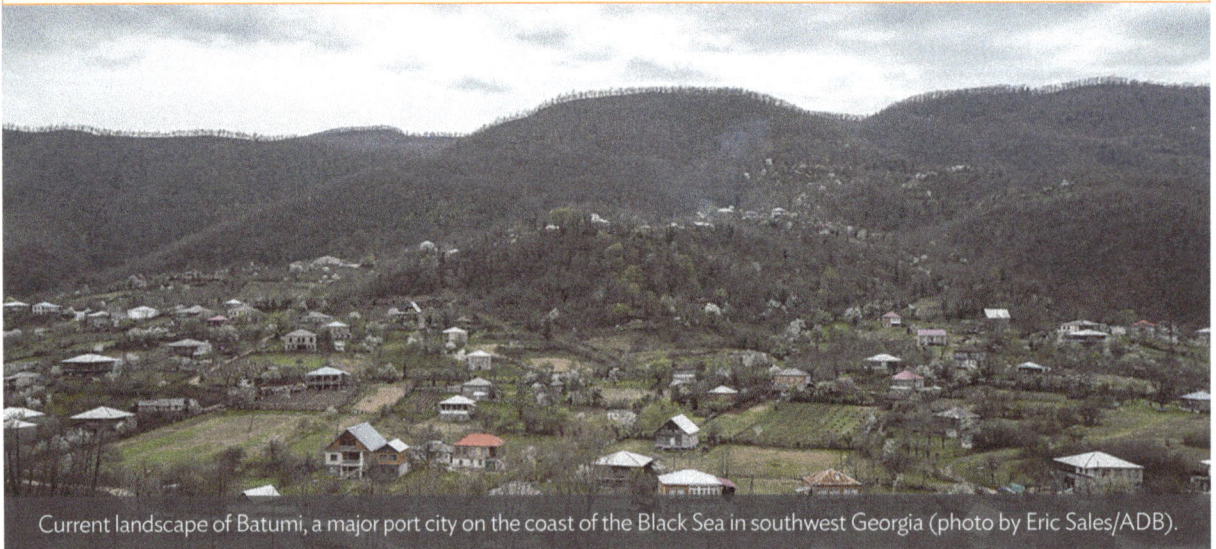

Current landscape of Batumi, a major port city on the coast of the Black Sea in southwest Georgia (photo by Eric Sales/ADB).

Table 2.1: Summary of National-Level Changes in Future Climate Under Medium and High Emissions Scenarios (Georgia)

Variable	Units [Δ units]	Historic	Δ RCP45 2030	Δ RCP45 2050	Δ RCP85 2030	Δ RCP85 2050
Average climate trends						
Mean Annual Temperature	°C [°C]	12.7	**1.3** [0.8, 1.8]	**1.9** [1.5, 2.5]	**1.4** [0.9, 2]	**2.7** [2, 3.4]
Total Annual Precipitation	mm/day [%]	939.9	**2.9** [(9.7), 12]	**0.7** [(9.2), 13.1]	**2.8** [(8.5), 14]	**(0.3)** [(11.1), 11.6]
Extreme temperature trends						
Maximum Annual Temperature	°C [°C]	31	**2** [0.8, 3.1]	**2.9** [1.8, 3.9]	**2.2** [1.1, 3.3]	**3.9** [2.7, 5.3]
Minimum Annual Temperature	°C [°C]	(18.8)	**1.1** [(1), 3.5]	**1.6** [(0.5), 3.8]	**1.6** [(1), 3.8]	**2.3** [(0.3), 4.6]
Extreme precipitation trends						
Maximum 1-Day Precipitation	mm/day [%]	44.1	**4** [(10.3), 19.8]	**3.6** [(12.2), 20.7]	**2** [(11.8), 19.9]	**4.6** [(11), 22.8]
Drought Period Length	days [days]	19	**0.8** [(2.1), 5.3]	**1.5** [(1.4), 5.7]	**1** [(2.3), 5.7]	**3.1** [(0.7), 8.8]

Δ = change, ( ) = negative, mm = millimeter, RCP = representative concentration pathway.

Notes: Numbers in brackets represent median values (25th percentile, 75th percentile) of climate model ensemble predictions.
          ERA5 refers to the 5th generation atmospheric reanalysis of the global climate, covering 1950 to the present.

Source: Asian Development Bank project team and consultant experts, using data from ERA5 (historical) and NASA Earth Exchange climate model projections (RCP45 and RCP85).

Shoreline rehabilitation and construction of a bypass road, under an ADB-financed program, helped protect the Black Sea coast and conserve the urban space in this area between Batumi and Kobuleti towns in southwestern Georgia (photo by Daro Sulakauri/ADB).

Figure 2.3: Seasonal Changes in Temperature and Precipitation, Historical and Future Time Horizons (Georgia)

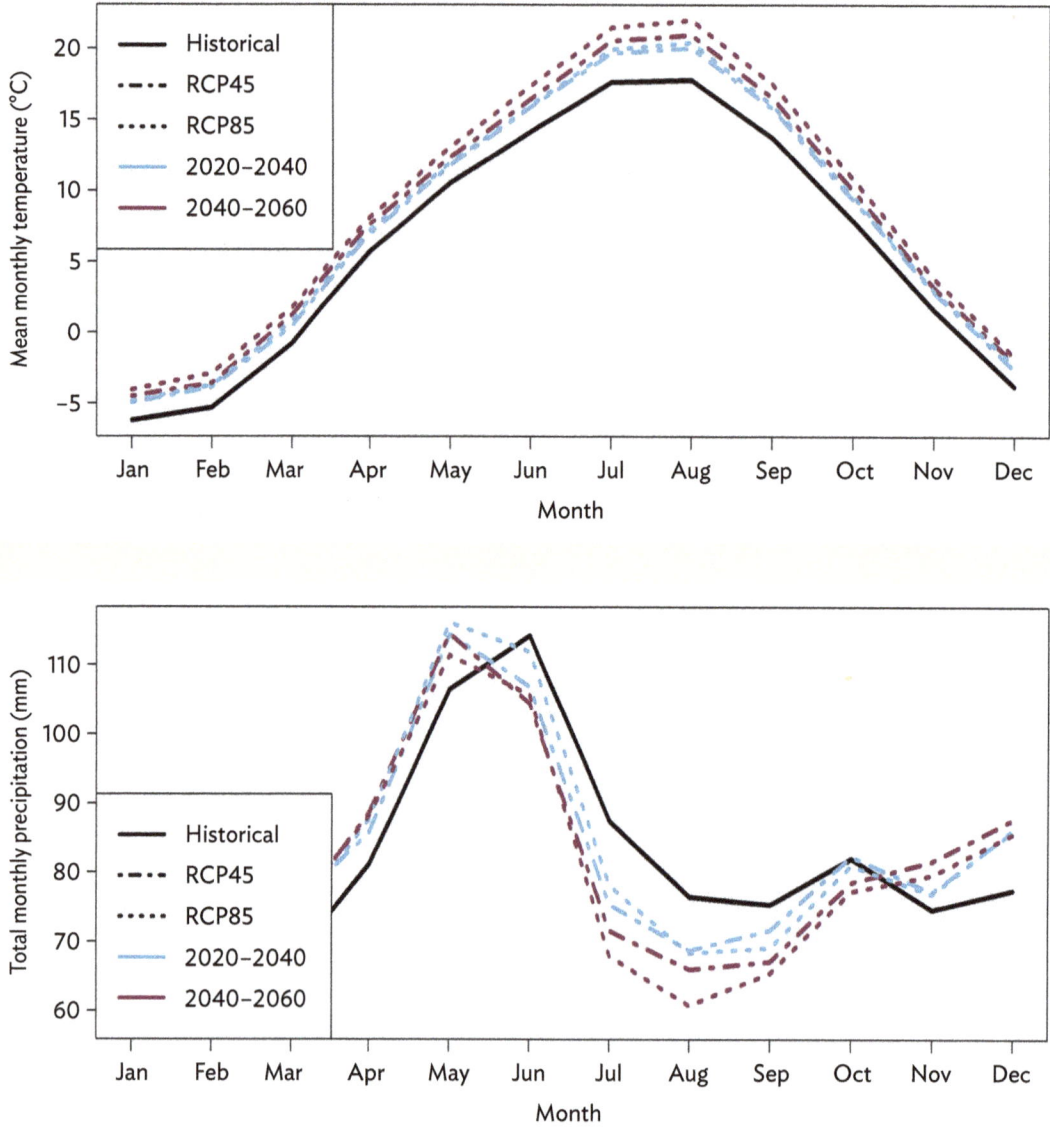

mm = millimeter, RCP = representative concentration pathway.

Notes: Historical data represent changes in total monthly precipitation in 1996–2015.
ERA5 refers to the 5th generation atmospheric reanalysis of the global climate, covering 1950 to the present.

Source: Asian Development Bank project team and consultant experts, using data from ERA5 (historical) and NASA Earth Exchange climate model projections (RCP45 and RCP85).

2.2 Climate Trends and Risk Analyses: Batumi (Ajaria Province)

SUMMARY (2050)

City-scale risk
- Limited risk of extreme heat events across area, increased for urban areas
- Moderate riverine flood risk along road networks, coastal and storm surge flood risks along coastline

National-scale hazards
- Unlikely to experience extreme water stress
- Extreme cold events are unlikely to affect area

Changes in climate
- Moderate increases in maximum yearly temperature will likely increase frequency and intensity of heat waves
- Small increases in maximum 1-day precipitation events may increase flood risk

Extreme precipitation
- The most severe precipitation events predicted by climate model ensemble are of extreme intensity

Sea-level rise
- Increases in sea level likely to increase coastal flood risk

Figure 2.4: Current Risk Associated with Extreme Heat and Riverine Flooding (Batumi)

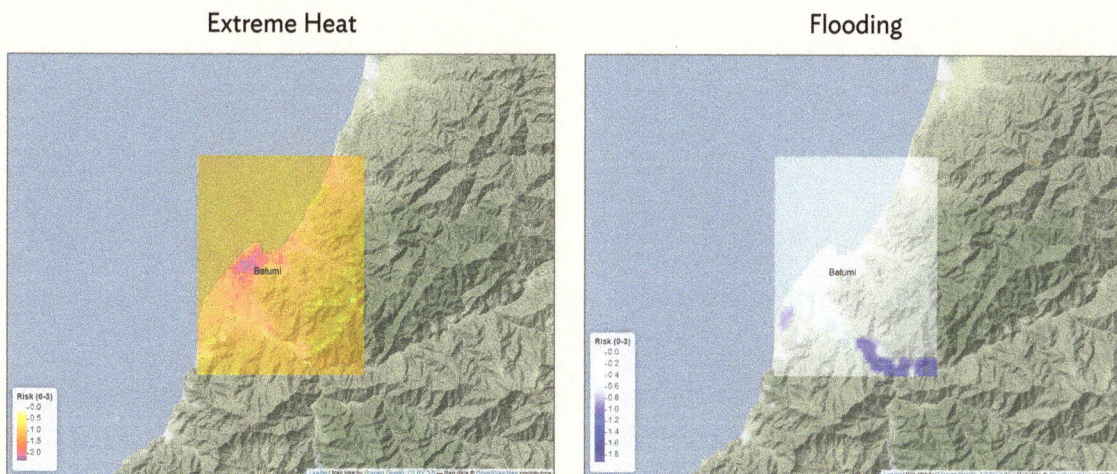

Note: 0 = no risk, 3 = high risk.

Source: Asian Development Bank project team and consultant experts, using data from the United Nations (population density and gross domestic product); OpenStreetMap (vulnerability of road networks, buildings, and points of interest); United Nations Office for Disaster Risk Reduction. 2015. *Global Assessment Report on Disaster Risk Reduction 2015.* Geneva (1 in 100-year flood hazard); and Google Earth Engine (heat anomaly signals).

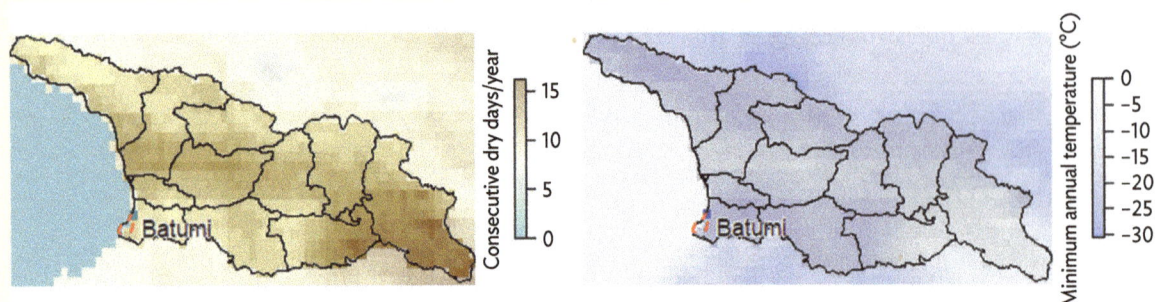

Figure 2.5: Current Hazards Associated with Water Shortage or Drought and Extreme Cold Events (Batumi)

Notes: Map shows the spatial distribution of each hazard and the location of the urban area in this context.
ERA5 refers to the 5th generation atmospheric reanalysis of the global climate, covering 1950 to the present.
Source: Asian Development Bank project team and consultant experts, using data from ERA5 (drought and extreme low temperature).

Table 2.2: Changes in Future Climate under Medium and High Emissions Scenarios (Batumi)

Variable	Units [Δ units]	Historic	Δ RCP45 2030	Δ RCP45 2050	Δ RCP85 2030	Δ RCP85 2050
Average climate trends						
Mean Annual Temperature	°C [°C]	13.4	1.3 [0.9, 1.8]	2 [1.5, 2.6]	1.5 [1, 2.1]	2.8 [2.1, 3.6]
Total Annual Precipitation	mm/year [%]	1,151.7	1.8 [(9.8), 12.4]	2 [(10.5), 13.9]	2.2 [(9.7), 14.4]	0.3 [(11.5), 13.5]
Extreme temperature trends						
Maximum Annual Temperature	°C [°C]	30.5	1.8 [0.6, 3]	2.6 [1.4, 3.9]	1.9 [0.7, 3.1]	3.7 [2.3, 5.2]
Minimum Annual Temperature	°C [°C]	(17.1)	1.2 [(1.3), 3.3]	1.6 [(0.4), 3.9]	1.6 [(0.8), 3.7]	2.6 [0.2, 4.6]
Extreme precipitation trends						
Maximum 1-Day Precipitation	mm/day [%]	52.4	3.3 [(15.8), 27.4]	3.1 [(15.5), 29.4]	1.4 [(16.2), 27.5]	6.1 [(13.1), 38.5]
Drought Period Length	days [days]	16.9	0.9 [(2.4), 5.4]	1.7 [(1.5), 6.5]	0.8 [(2.7), 5.9]	3.2 [(0.8), 8.4]
Sea-level rise						
Projected Sea-Level Rise	m		0.21 [0.15, 0.27]	0.41 [0.32, 0.5]	0.22 [0.17, 0.27]	0.44 [0.35, 0.53]

Δ = change, ( ) = negative, m = meter, mm = millimeter, RCP = representative concentration pathway.
Notes: Numbers in brackets represent median values (25th percentile, 75th percentile) of climate model ensemble predictions.
ERA5 refers to the 5th generation atmospheric reanalysis of the global climate, covering 1950 to the present.
Source: Asian Development Bank project team and consultant experts, using data from ERA5 (historical) and NASA Earth Exchange climate model projections (RCP45 and RCP85).

Figure 2.6: Return Period Analysis of Extreme Precipitation Events (Batumi)

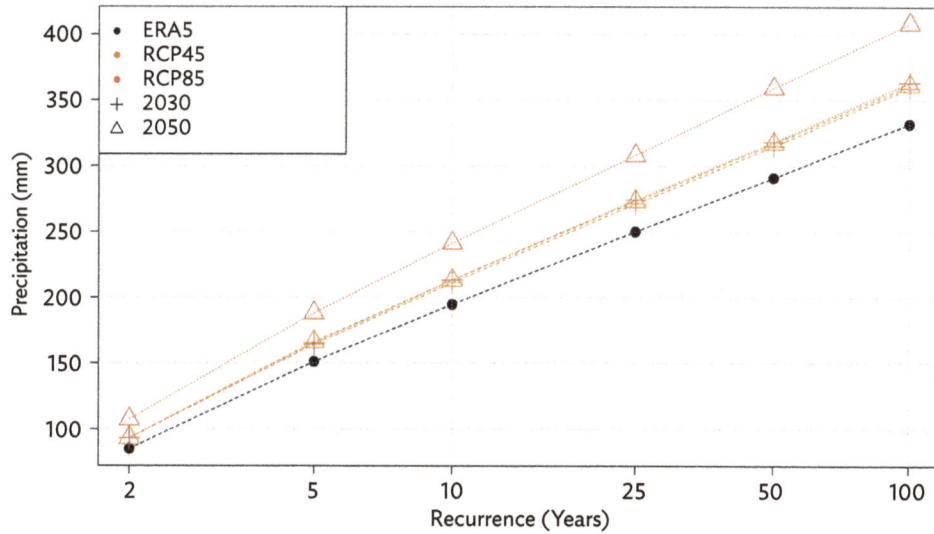

	Return Period					
	2 Years	5 Years	10 Years	25 Years	50 Years	100 Years
Historical daily maximum precipitation (mm)						
ERA5	85	151	195	250	291	332
Future (75th percentile of GCM distribution) (mm)						
RCP45 2030	93	164	211	271	315	359
RCP45 2050	93	166	213	273	317	361
RCP85 2030	93	165	213	274	318	363
RCP85 2050	107	188	241	308	359	408

Δ = change, GCM = global circulation model, mm = millimeter, RCP = representative concentration pathway.

Notes: The analysis represents changes in the yearly maximum 1-day precipitation (Rx1day) at various return periods, providing predictions of future frequencies of extreme precipitation events. It is based on the third quartile (75th percentile) of ensemble predictions and uses a Gumbel fitting approach to estimate the extreme events. The numbers can be used to inform the design of more climate-resilient urban infrastructure.

ERA5 refers to the 5th generation atmospheric reanalysis of the global climate, covering 1950 to the present.

Source: Asian Development Bank project team and consultant experts, using data from ERA5 (historical) and NASA Earth Exchange climate model projections (RCP45 and RCP85).

2.3 Climate Trends and Risk Analyses: Gori (Shida Kartli Province)

SUMMARY (2050)

City-scale risk
- Moderate risk of extreme heat events across area, increased risk in urban center
- High riverine flood risk in urban center, along road networks

National-scale hazards
- Unlikely to experience extreme water stress problems
- Extreme cold events are unlikely to affect area

Changes in climate
- Large increases in maximum yearly temperature will likely increase frequency and intensity of heat waves
- Small increases in maximum 1-day precipitation events may increase flood risk

Extreme precipitation
- The most severe precipitation events predicted by climate model ensemble are of high intensity

Figure 2.7: Current Risk Associated with Extreme Heat and Riverine Flooding (Gori)

Extreme Heat

Flooding

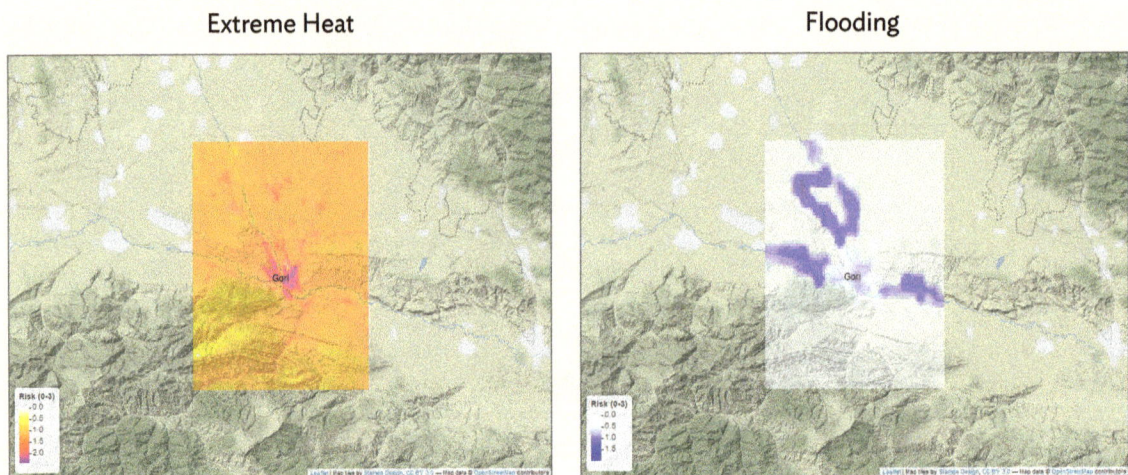

Note: 0 = no risk, 3 = high risk.

Source: Asian Development Bank project team and consultant experts, using data from the United Nations (population density and gross domestic product); OpenStreetMap (vulnerability of road networks, buildings, and points of interest); United Nations Office for Disaster Risk Reduction. 2015. *Global Assessment Report on Disaster Risk Reduction 2015*. Geneva (1 in 100-year flood hazard); and Google Earth Engine (heat anomaly signals).

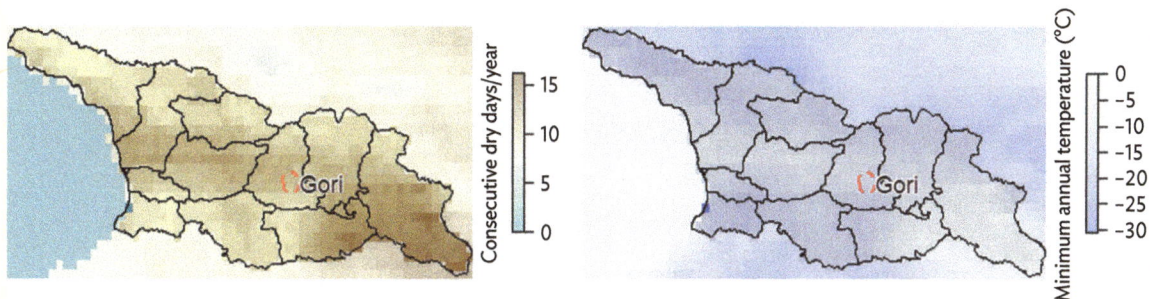

Figure 2.8: Current Hazards Associated with Water Shortage or Drought and Extreme Cold Events (Gori)

Notes: Map shows the spatial distribution of each hazard and the location of the urban area in this context.
ERA5 refers to the 5th generation atmospheric reanalysis of the global climate, covering 1950 to the present.

Source: Asian Development Bank project team and consultant experts, using data from ERA5 (drought and extreme low temperature).

Table 2.3: Changes in Future Climate under Medium and High Emissions Scenarios (Gori)

Variable	Units [Δ units]	Historic	Δ RCP45 2030	Δ RCP45 2050	Δ RCP85 2030	Δ RCP85 2050
Average climate trends						
Mean Annual Temperature	°C [°C]	12.4	**1.3** [0.8, 1.9]	**2** [1.5, 2.6]	**1.5** [0.9, 2.1]	**2.9** [2.1, 3.5]
Total Annual Precipitation	mm/year [%]	825.9	**2.8** [(9.7), 13.1]	**0.7** [(10.7), 14.7]	**3.3** [(9.4), 14.7]	**(0.7)** [(13), 13.1]
Extreme temperature trends						
Maximum Annual Temperature	°C [°C]	31.5	**2** [0.8, 3.3]	**3.1** [1.8, 4.4]	**2.3** [1, 3.6]	**4.1** [2.8, 5.6]
Minimum Annual Temperature	°C [°C]	(21.2)	**1.1** [(1.2), 3.8]	**1.7** [(0.4), 4.3]	**1.7** [(1.2), 4]	**2.3** [(0.3), 4.8]
Extreme precipitation trends						
Maximum 1-Day Precipitation	mm/day [%]	36.8	**3.6** [(13.5), 23.4]	**0.4** [(16.7), 24]	**1.4** [(16.5), 20.2]	**4.9** [(13.4), 28.1]
Drought Period Length	days [days]	18.7	**1** [(2.8), 5.9]	**1.3** [(2.1), 6.3]	**1.3** [(2.8), 6.7]	**3.2** [(1.6), 8.8]

Δ = change, ( ) = negative, mm = millimeter, RCP = representative concentration pathway.

Notes: Numbers in brackets represent median values (25th percentile, 75th percentile) of climate model ensemble predictions.
ERA5 refers to the 5th generation atmospheric reanalysis of the global climate, covering 1950 to the present.

Source: Asian Development Bank project team and consultant experts, using data from ERA5 (historical) and NASA Earth Exchange climate model projections (RCP45 and RCP85).

Figure 2.9: Return Period Analysis of Extreme Precipitation Events (Gori)

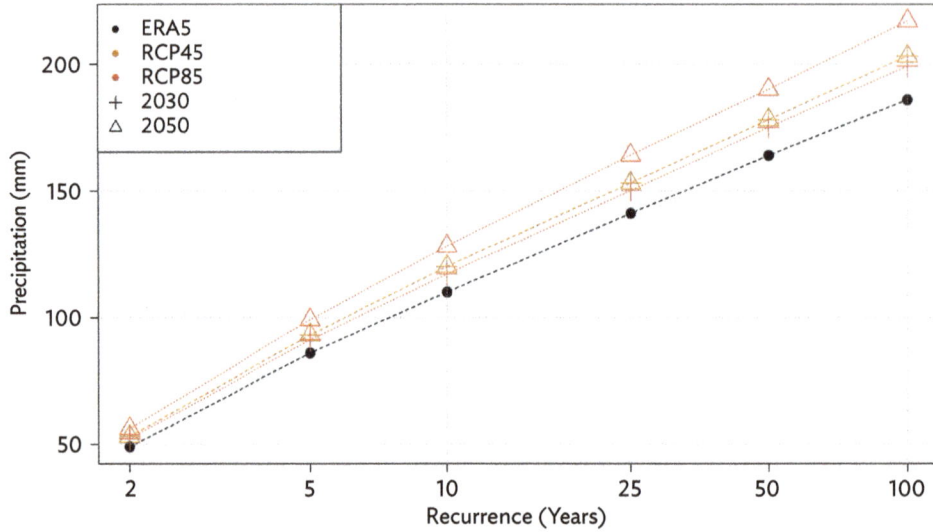

	2 Years	5 Years	10 Years	25 Years	50 Years	100 Years
Historical daily maximum precipitation (mm)						
ERA5	49	86	110	141	164	186
Future (75th percentile of GCM distribution) (mm)						
RCP45 2030	53	93	120	153	178	203
RCP45 2050	53	93	120	153	178	203
RCP85 2030	52	91	117	150	175	199
RCP85 2050	56	99	128	164	190	217

Δ = change, GCM = global circulation model, mm = millimeter, RCP = representative concentration pathway.

Notes: The analysis represents changes in the yearly maximum 1-day precipitation (Rx1day) at various return periods, providing predictions of future frequencies of extreme precipitation events. It is based on the third quartile (75th percentile) of ensemble predictions and uses a Gumbel fitting approach to estimate the extreme events. The numbers can be used to inform the design of more climate-resilient urban infrastructure.

ERA5 refers to the 5th generation atmospheric reanalysis of the global climate, covering 1950 to the present.

Source: Asian Development Bank project team and consultant experts, using data from ERA5 (historical) and NASA Earth Exchange climate model projections (RCP45 and RCP85).

2.4 Climate Trends and Risk Analyses: Kutaisi (Imereti Province)

SUMMARY (2050)

City-scale risk
- Moderate risk of extreme heat events across area, increased risk in urban center
- Moderate riverine flood risk in urban center, along road networks

National-scale hazards
- Unlikely to experience extreme water stress problems
- Extreme cold events are unlikely to affect area

Changes in climate
- Moderate increases in maximum yearly temperature will likely increase frequency and intensity of heat waves
- Moderate increases in maximum 1-day precipitation events may increase flood risk

Extreme precipitation
- The most severe precipitation events predicted by climate model ensemble are of high intensity

Figure 2.10: Current Risk Associated with Extreme Heat and Riverine Flooding (Kutaisi)

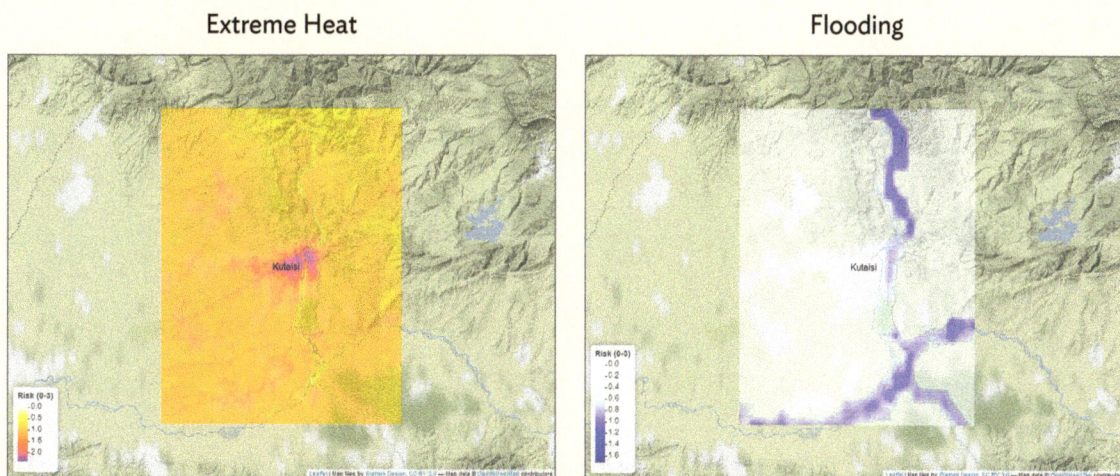

Note: 0 = no risk, 3 = high risk.

Source: Asian Development Bank project team and consultant experts, using data from the United Nations (population density and gross domestic product); OpenStreetMap (vulnerability of road networks, buildings, and points of interest); United Nations Office for Disaster Risk Reduction. 2015. *Global Assessment Report on Disaster Risk Reduction 2015*. Geneva (1 in 100-year flood hazard); and Google Earth Engine (heat anomaly signals).

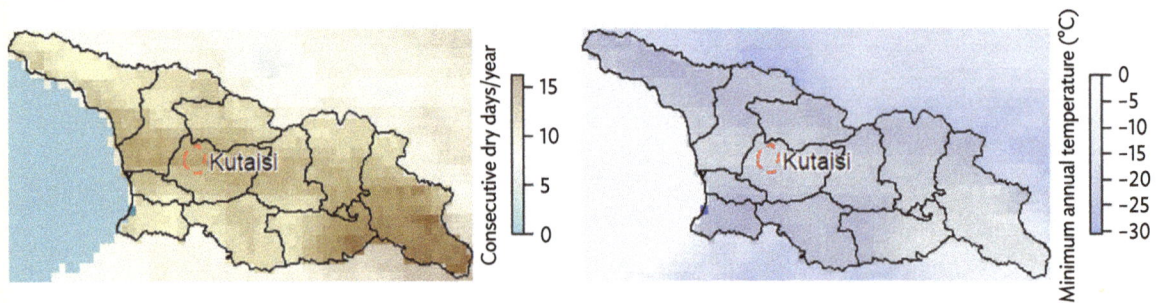

Figure 2.11: Current Hazards Associated with Water Shortage or Drought and Extreme Cold Events (Kutaisi)

Notes: Map shows the spatial distribution of each hazard and the location of the urban area in this context.
ERA5 refers to the 5th generation atmospheric reanalysis of the global climate, covering 1950 to the present.

Source: Asian Development Bank project team and consultant experts, using data from ERA5 (drought and extreme low temperature).

Table 2.4: Changes in Future Climate under Medium and High Emissions Scenarios (Kutaisi)

Variable	Units [Δ units]	Historic	Δ RCP45 2030	Δ RCP45 2050	Δ RCP85 2030	Δ RCP85 2050
Average climate trends						
Mean Annual Temperature	°C [°C]	15.3	1.3 [0.8, 1.8]	2 [1.5, 2.6]	1.5 [0.9, 2.1]	2.8 [2, 3.5]
Total Annual Precipitation	mm/year [%]	993.4	2.5 [(9.2), 13.2]	1.2 [(9.4), 14.9]	2.7 [(7.9), 14.5]	0.2 [(11.1), 12.5]
Extreme temperature trends						
Maximum Annual Temperature	°C [°C]	32.9	1.8 [0.6, 3.1]	2.8 [1.6, 4.2]	2 [0.8, 3.5]	3.8 [2.5, 5.6]
Minimum Annual Temperature	°C [°C]	(16.4)	1 [(1.4), 3.5]	1.6 [(0.7), 3.9]	1.5 [(1.2), 3.8]	2.3 [(0.4), 4.8]
Extreme precipitation trends						
Maximum 1-Day Precipitation	mm/day [%]	42.4	3.9 [(13.6), 25]	3.3 [(12), 29.2]	4.7 [(14.7), 29.6]	7 [(12.1), 34.6]
Drought Period Length	days [days]	17.1	1.1 [(2.1), 6.1]	1.8 [(1.7), 6.8]	1.4 [(2.6), 6.1]	3.4 [(0.8), 8.9]

Δ = change, ( ) = negative, mm = millimeter, RCP = representative concentration pathway.

Notes: Numbers in brackets represent median values (25th percentile, 75th percentile) of climate model ensemble predictions.
ERA5 refers to the 5th generation atmospheric reanalysis of the global climate, covering 1950 to the present.

Source: Asian Development Bank project team and consultant experts, using data from ERA5 (historical) and NASA Earth Exchange climate model projections (RCP45 and RCP85).

Figure 2.12: Return Period Analysis of Extreme Precipitation Events (Kutaisi)

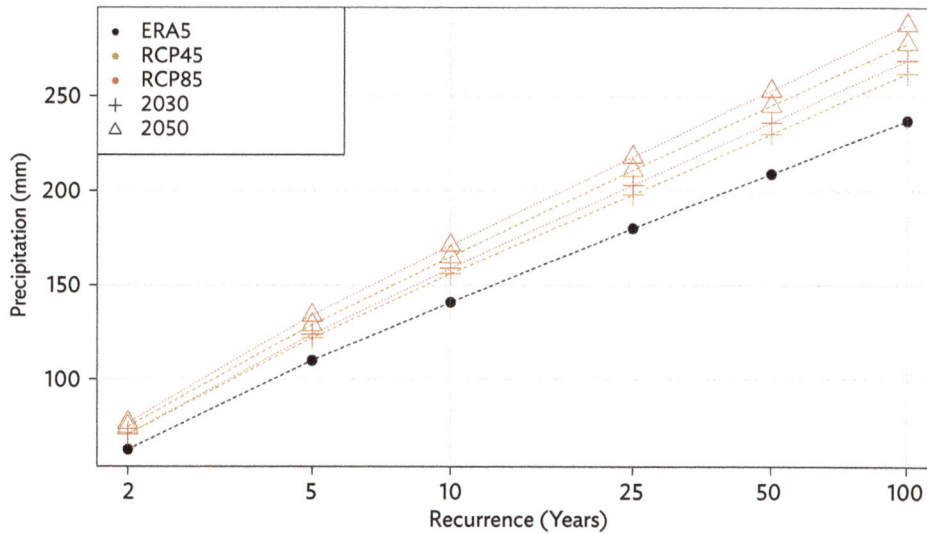

	Return Period					
	2 Years	5 Years	10 Years	25 Years	50 Years	100 Years
Historical daily maximum precipitation (mm)						
ERA5	63	110	141	180	209	237
Future (75th percentile of GCM distribution) (mm)						
RCP45 2030	71	122	156	198	230	262
RCP45 2050	75	129	165	211	245	278
RCP85 2030	71	124	159	203	236	269
RCP85 2050	77	134	171	218	253	288

Δ = change, GCM = global circulation model, mm = millimeter, RCP = representative concentration pathway.

Notes: The analysis represents changes in the yearly maximum 1-day precipitation (Rx1day) at various return periods, providing predictions of future frequencies of extreme precipitation events. It is based on the third quartile (75th percentile) of ensemble predictions and uses a Gumbel fitting approach to estimate the extreme events. The numbers can be used to inform the design of more climate-resilient urban infrastructure.

ERA5 refers to the 5th generation atmospheric reanalysis of the global climate, covering 1950 to the present.

Source: Asian Development Bank project team and consultant experts, using data from ERA5 (historical) and NASA Earth Exchange climate model projections (RCP45 and RCP85).

2.5 Climate Trends and Risk Analyses: Mestia–Lentekhi (Samegrelo–Zemo Svaneti Province)

SUMMARY (2050)

City-scale risk
- Limited risk of extreme heat events across area, increased risk in urban center
- Moderate riverine flood risk along road networks

National-scale hazards
- Unlikely to experience extreme water stress problems
- Extreme cold events are most likely to affect north of area

Changes in climate
- Large increases in maximum yearly temperature will likely increase frequency and intensity of heat waves
- Moderate increases in maximum 1-day precipitation events may increase flood risk

Extreme precipitation
- The most severe precipitation events predicted by climate model ensemble are of high intensity

Figure 2.13: Current Risk Associated with Extreme Heat and Riverine Flooding (Mestia–Lentekhi)

Extreme Heat

Flooding

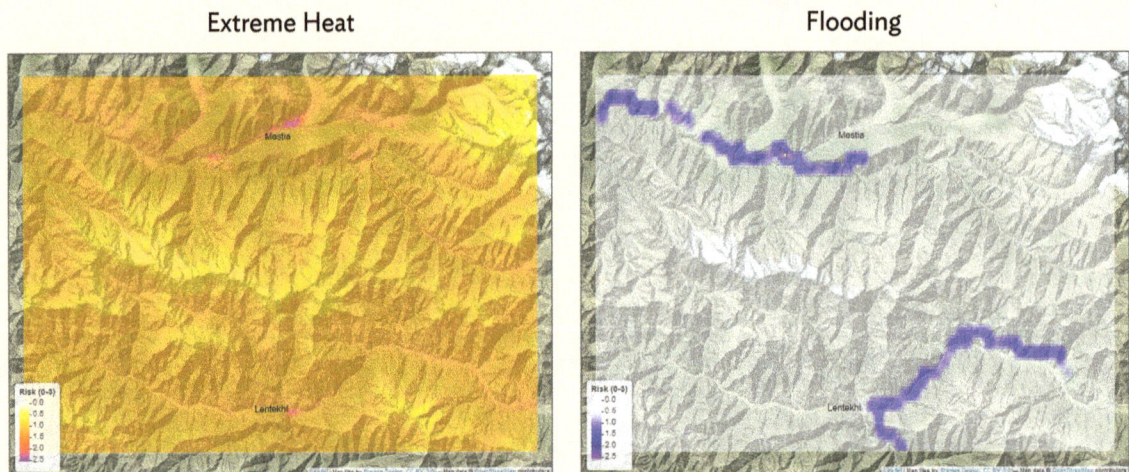

Note: 0 = no risk, 3 = high risk.

Source: Asian Development Bank project team and consultant experts, using data from the United Nations (population density and gross domestic product); OpenStreetMap (vulnerability of road networks, buildings, and points of interest); United Nations Office for Disaster Risk Reduction. 2015. *Global Assessment Report on Disaster Risk Reduction 2015*. Geneva (1 in 100-year flood hazard); and Google Earth Engine (heat anomaly signals).

Figure 2.14: Current Hazards Associated with Water Shortage or Drought and Extreme Cold Events (Mestia–Lentekhi)

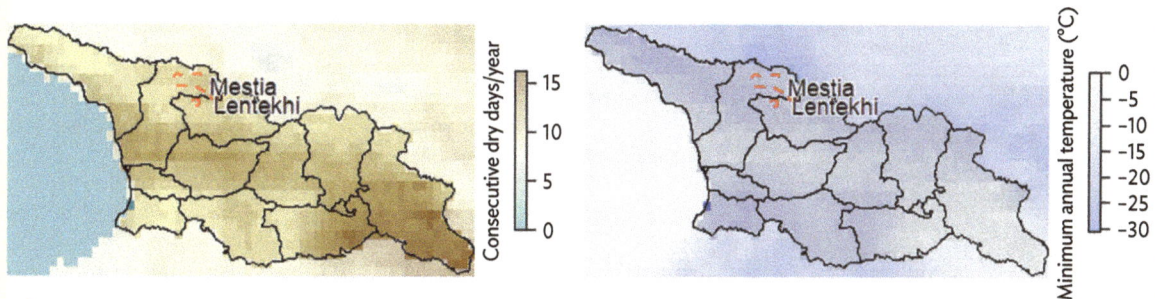

Notes: Map shows the spatial distribution of each hazard and the location of the urban area in this context.
ERA5 refers to the 5th generation atmospheric reanalysis of the global climate, covering 1950 to the present.

Source: Asian Development Bank project team and consultant experts, using data from ERA5 (drought and extreme low temperature).

Table 2.5: Changes in Future Climate under Medium and High Emissions Scenarios (Mestia–Lentekhi)

Variable	Units [Δ units]	Historic	Δ RCP45 2030	Δ RCP45 2050	Δ RCP85 2030	Δ RCP85 2050
Average climate trends						
Mean Annual Temperature	°C [°C]	10	**1.3** [0.8, 1.8]	**1.9** [1.5, 2.5]	**1.5** [0.9, 2.1]	**2.7** [2, 3.5]
Total Annual Precipitation	mm/year [%]	992.5	**3.2** [(10), 13.4]	**1.2** [(9.4), 14.3]	**2.8** [(7.6), 15.1]	**0.2** [(10.9), 14]
Extreme temperature trends						
Maximum Annual Temperature	°C [°C]	28.8	**1.8** [0.6, 3.2]	**2.8** [1.6, 4.1]	**2.1** [0.9, 3.4]	**3.8** [2.6, 5.5]
Minimum Annual Temperature	°C [°C]	(22.9)	**1.2** [(1.6), 3.6]	**1.5** [(0.8), 4.2]	**1.4** [(1.1), 3.8]	**2.3** [(0.7), 4.8]
Extreme precipitation trends						
Maximum 1-Day Precipitation	mm/day [%]	41.9	**6.8** [(9.1), 28.6]	**6.9** [(11.2), 26.7]	**5.9** [(13.5), 29.1]	**8.3** [(10.6), 35.1]
Drought Period Length	days [days]	17	**1** [(2.2), 6.3]	**1.6** [(1.8), 6.1]	**1.4** [(2.6), 5.8]	**3.1** [(0.9), 8.6]

Δ = change, ( ) = negative, mm = millimeter, RCP = representative concentration pathway.

Notes: Numbers in brackets represent median values (25th percentile, 75th percentile) of climate model ensemble predictions.
ERA5 refers to the 5th generation atmospheric reanalysis of the global climate, covering 1950 to the present.

Source: Asian Development Bank project team and consultant experts, using data from ERA5 (historical) and NASA Earth Exchange climate model projections (RCP45 and RCP85).

Figure 2.15: Return Period Analysis of Extreme Precipitation Events (Mestia–Lentekhi)

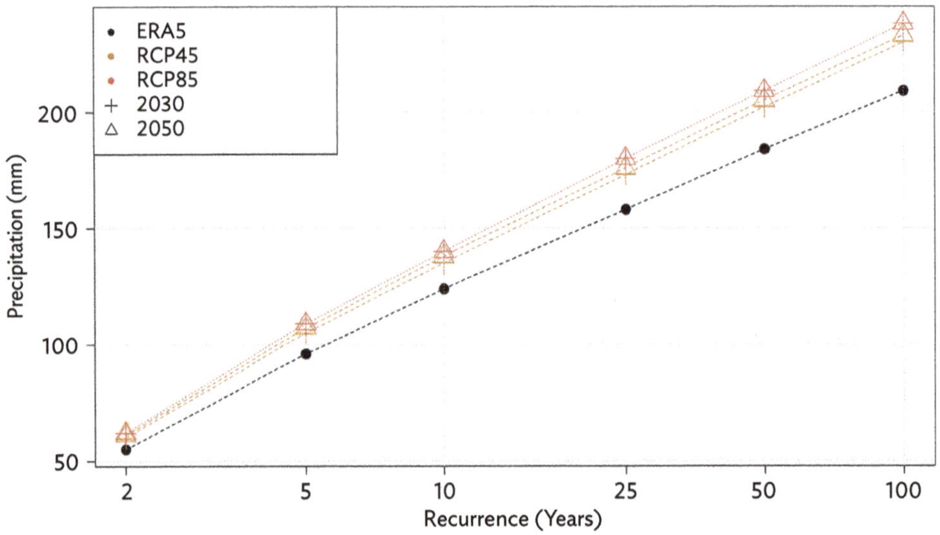

	Return Period					
	2 Years	**5 Years**	**10 Years**	**25 Years**	**50 Years**	**100 Years**
Historical daily maximum precipitation (mm)						
ERA5	55	96	124	158	184	209
Future (75th percentile of GCM distribution) (mm)						
RCP45 2030	60	105	135	173	202	230
RCP45 2050	61	107	138	176	205	233
RCP85 2030	62	109	140	180	209	238
RCP85 2050	62	109	140	180	209	238

Δ = change, GCM = global circulation model, mm = millimeter, RCP = representative concentration pathway.

Notes: The analysis represents changes in the yearly maximum 1-day precipitation (Rx1day) at various return periods, providing predictions of future frequencies of extreme precipitation events. It is based on the third quartile (75th percentile) of ensemble predictions and uses a Gumbel fitting approach to estimate the extreme events. The numbers can be used to inform the design of more climate-resilient urban infrastructure.

ERA5 refers to the 5th generation atmospheric reanalysis of the global climate, covering 1950 to the present.

Source: Asian Development Bank project team and consultant experts, using data from ERA5 (historical) and NASA Earth Exchange climate model projections (RCP45 and RCP85).

2.6 Climate Trends and Risk Analyses: Northern Kakheti (Kakheti Province)

SUMMARY (2050)

City-scale risk
- Limited risk of extreme heat events across area, increased risk in urban center
- Moderate riverine flood risk along road networks

National-scale hazards
- Unlikely to experience extreme water stress problems
- Extreme cold events are most likely to affect north of area

Changes in climate
- Large increases in maximum yearly temperature will likely increase frequency and intensity of heat waves
- Moderate increases in maximum 1-day precipitation events may increase flood risk

Extreme precipitation
- The most severe precipitation events predicted by climate model ensemble are of high intensity

Figure 2.16: Current Risk Associated with Extreme Heat and Riverine Flooding (Northern Kakheti)

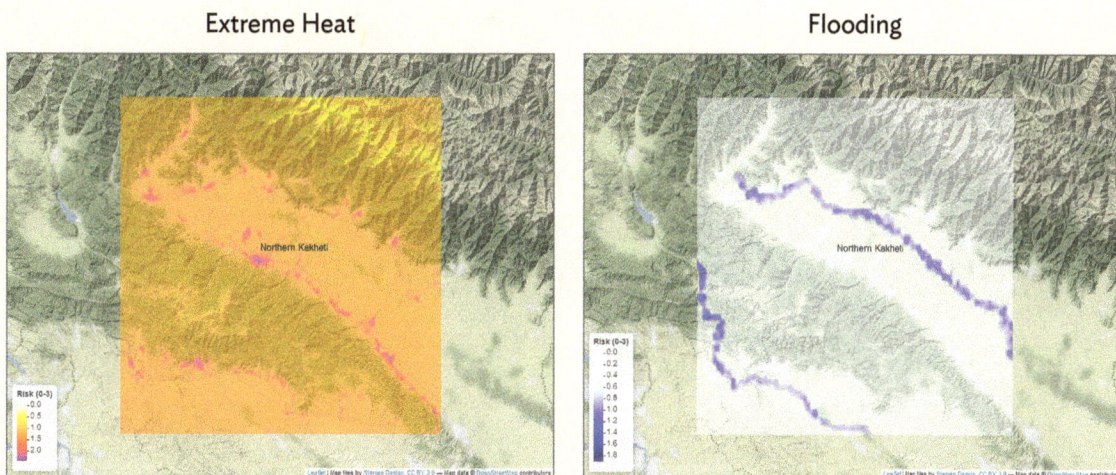

Note: 0 = no risk, 3 = high risk.

Source: Asian Development Bank project team and consultant experts, using data from the United Nations (population density and gross domestic product); OpenStreetMap (vulnerability of road networks, buildings, and points of interest); United Nations Office for Disaster Risk Reduction. 2015. *Global Assessment Report on Disaster Risk Reduction 2015*. Geneva (1 in 100-year flood hazard); and Google Earth Engine (heat anomaly signals).

Figure 2.17: Current Hazards Associated with Water Shortage or Drought and Extreme Cold Events (Northern Kakheti)

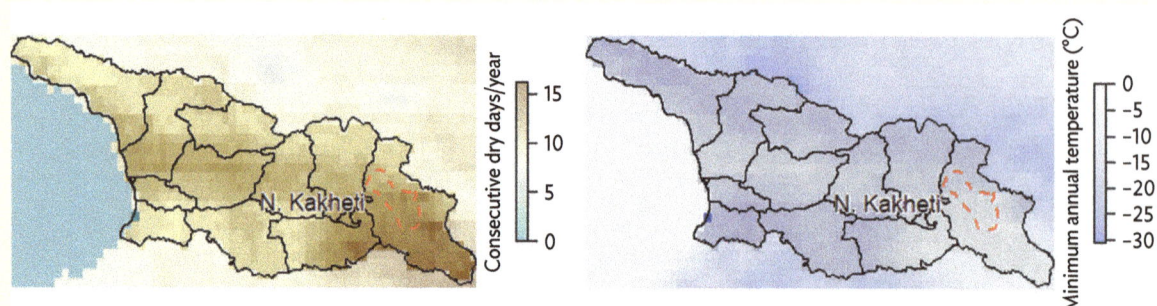

N. Kakheti = Northern Kakheti.

Notes: Map shows the spatial distribution of each hazard and the location of the urban area in this context.
       ERA5 refers to the 5th generation atmospheric reanalysis of the global climate, covering 1950 to the present.

Source: Asian Development Bank project team and consultant experts, using data from ERA5 (drought and extreme low temperature).

Table 2.6: Changes in Future Climate under Medium and High Emissions Scenarios (Northern Kakheti)

Variable	Units [Δ units]	Historic	Δ RCP45 2030	Δ RCP45 2050	Δ RCP85 2030	Δ RCP85 2050
Average climate trends						
Mean Annual Temperature	°C [°C]	14.6	**1.3** [0.7, 1.8]	**2.1** [1.5, 2.6]	**1.5** [0.8, 2.1]	**2.8** [2, 3.4]
Total Annual Precipitation	mm/year [%]	702.5	**1.6** [(8.3), 13.9]	**0.3** [(11.3), 13.4]	**1.8** [(11.8), 15.1]	**(1.7)** [(15.4), 12.5]
Extreme temperature trends						
Maximum Annual Temperature	°C [°C]	33.3	**2.1** [0.9, 3.3]	**3.2** [1.9, 4.4]	**2.4** [1.3, 3.5]	**4.1** [2.9, 5.4]
Minimum Annual Temperature	°C [°C]	(16.0)	**1.1** [(1.3), 3.3]	**1.5** [(0.8), 3.5]	**1.5** [(1.3), 3.7]	**2** [(0.6), 4.2]
Extreme precipitation trends						
Maximum 1-Day Precipitation	mm/day [%]	36.3	**7.8** [(13.3), 28.8]	**4.9** [(15.6), 28.9]	**4.1** [(16.4), 27.7]	**7.4** [(15.2), 35.4]
Drought Period Length	days [days]	21.8	**0.6** [(3.3), 6.3]	**1.3** [(3), 7.4]	**1.4** [(3.2), 7.1]	**3.3** [(1.2), 9.7]

Δ = change, ( ) = negative, mm = millimeter, RCP = representative concentration pathway.

Notes: Numbers in brackets represent median values (25th percentile, 75th percentile) of climate model ensemble predictions.
       ERA5 refers to the 5th generation atmospheric reanalysis of the global climate, covering 1950 to the present.

Source: Asian Development Bank project team and consultant experts, using data from ERA5 (historical) and NASA Earth Exchange climate model projections (RCP45 and RCP85).

Figure 2.18: Return Period Analysis of Extreme Precipitation Events (Northern Kakheti)

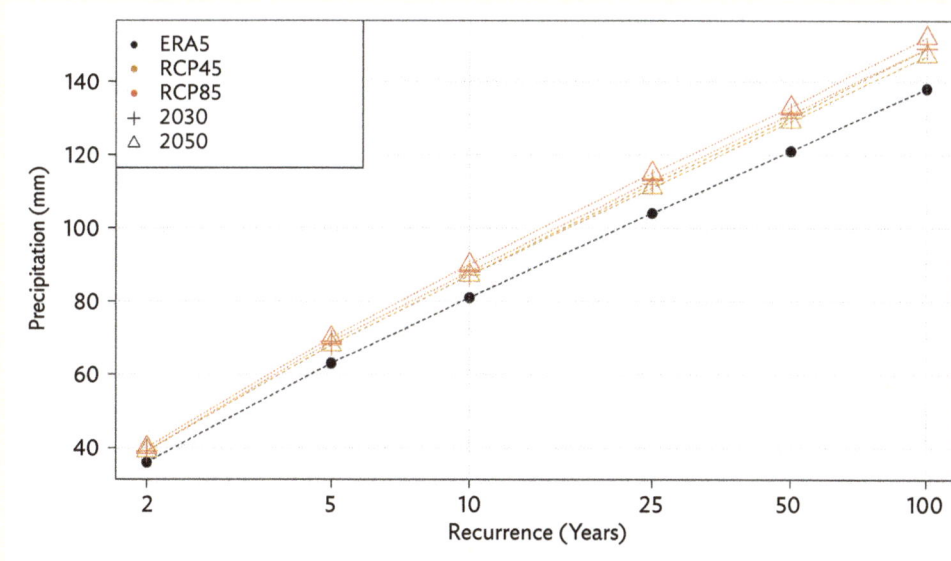

	Return Period					
	2 Years	**5 Years**	**10 Years**	**25 Years**	**50 Years**	**100 Years**
Historical daily maximum precipitation (mm)						
ERA5	36	63	81	104	121	138
Future (75th percentile of GCM distribution) (mm)						
RCP45 2030	39	68	87	112	130	149
RCP45 2050	39	68	87	111	129	147
RCP85 2030	39	69	88	113	131	149
RCP85 2050	40	70	90	115	133	152

Δ = change, GCM = global circulation model, mm = millimeter, RCP = representative concentration pathway.

Notes: The analysis represents changes in the yearly maximum 1-day precipitation (Rx1day) at various return periods, providing predictions of future frequencies of extreme precipitation events. It is based on the third quartile (75th percentile) of ensemble predictions and uses a Gumbel fitting approach to estimate the extreme events. The numbers can be used to inform the design of more climate-resilient urban infrastructure.

ERA5 refers to the 5th generation atmospheric reanalysis of the global climate, covering 1950 to the present.

Source: Asian Development Bank project team and consultant experts, using data from ERA5 (historical) and NASA Earth Exchange climate model projections (RCP45 and RCP85).

2.7 Climate Trends and Risk Analyses: Poti (Samegrelo–Zemo Svaneti Province)

SUMMARY (2050)

City-scale risk
- Limited risk of extreme heat events across area, increased risk in urban center
- Moderate riverine flood risk along road networks, coastal and storm surge flood risks along coastline

National-scale hazards
- Unlikely to experience extreme water stress
- Extreme cold events are unlikely to affect area

Changes in climate
- Moderate increases in maximum yearly temperature will likely increase frequency and intensity of heat waves
- Moderate increases in maximum 1-day precipitation events may increase flood risk

Extreme precipitation
- The most severe precipitation events predicted by climate model ensemble are of high intensity

Sea-level rise
- Increases in sea level likely to increase coastal flood risk

Figure 2.19: Current Risk Associated with Extreme Heat and Riverine Flooding (Poti)

Extreme Heat

Flooding

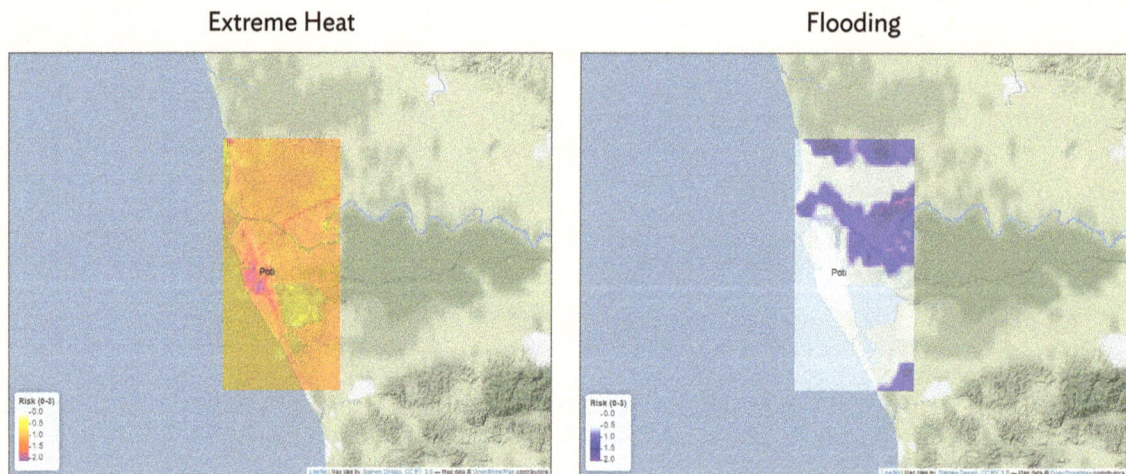

Note: 0 = no risk, 3 = high risk.

Source: Asian Development Bank project team and consultant experts, using data from the United Nations (population density and gross domestic product); OpenStreetMap (vulnerability of road networks, buildings, and points of interest); United Nations Office for Disaster Risk Reduction. 2015. *Global Assessment Report on Disaster Risk Reduction 2015*. Geneva (1 in 100-year flood hazard); and Google Earth Engine (heat anomaly signals).

Figure 2.20: Current Hazards Associated with Water Shortage or Drought and Extreme Cold Events (Poti)

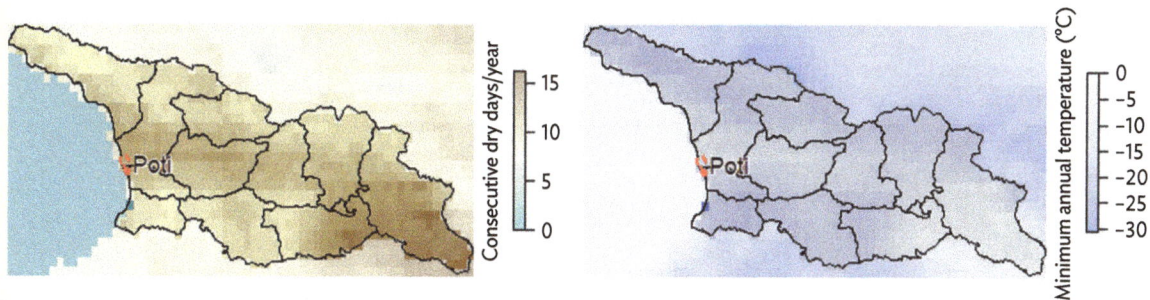

Notes: Map shows the spatial distribution of each hazard and the location of the urban area in this context.
ERA5 refers to the 5th generation atmospheric reanalysis of the global climate, covering 1950 to the present.

Source: Asian Development Bank project team and consultant experts, using data from ERA5 (drought and extreme low temperature).

Table 2.7: Changes in Future Climate under Medium and High Emissions Scenarios (Poti)

Variable	Units [Δ units]	Historic	Δ RCP45 2030	Δ RCP45 2050	Δ RCP85 2030	Δ RCP85 2050
Average climate trends						
Mean Annual Temperature	°C [°C]	16.2	1.3 [0.8, 1.8]	1.9 [1.4, 2.5]	1.5 [1, 2.1]	2.7 [2, 3.5]
Total Annual Precipitation	mm/year [%]	1,367.9	2.2 [(9.1), 13.7]	2.6 [(10.1), 15.1]	3.3 [(9.5), 14.6]	0.7 [(11.4), 14.4]
Extreme temperature trends						
Maximum Annual Temperature	°C [°C]	32.1	1.9 [0.7, 3]	2.6 [1.5, 3.9]	2 [0.8, 3.2]	3.7 [2.4, 5.2]
Minimum Annual Temperature	°C [°C]	(12.8)	1.3 [(1.3), 3.5]	1.7 [(0.4), 4.1]	1.7 [(0.7), 3.8]	2.6 [0, 4.7]
Extreme precipitation trends						
Maximum 1-Day Precipitation	mm/day [%]	61.6	5.3 [(14.8), 30.2]	6.5 [(12.1), 31.5]	5.9 [(13.3), 31.5]	8.6 [(11.3), 38.4]
Drought Period Length	days [days]	15.4	1 [(2), 5.3]	1.9 [(1.3), 6.1]	0.7 [(2.3), 5.4]	3.1 [(0.4), 8.1]
Sea-level rise						
Projected Sea-Level Rise	m		0.21 [0.15, 0.27]	0.41 [0.32, 0.5]	0.22 [0.17, 0.27]	0.44 [0.35, 0.53]

Δ = change, ( ) = negative, m = meter, mm = millimeter, RCP = representative concentration pathway.

Notes: Numbers in brackets represent median values (25th percentile, 75th percentile) of climate model ensemble predictions.
ERA5 refers to the 5th generation atmospheric reanalysis of the global climate, covering 1950 to the present.

Source: Asian Development Bank project team and consultant experts, using data from ERA5 (historical) and NASA Earth Exchange climate model projections (RCP45 and RCP85).

Figure 2.21: Return Period Analysis of Extreme Precipitation Events (Poti)

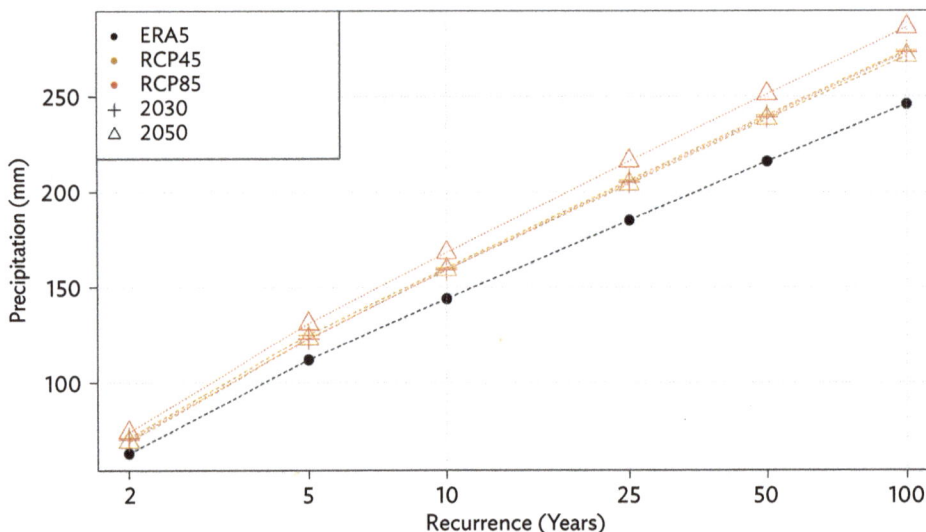

	Return Period					
	2 Years	5 Years	10 Years	25 Years	50 Years	100 Years
Historical daily maximum precipitation (mm)						
ERA5	63	112	144	185	216	246
Future (75th percentile of GCM distribution) (mm)						
RCP45 2030	71	125	160	206	240	274
RCP45 2050	69	123	159	204	238	271
RCP85 2030	70	123	159	205	239	273
RCP85 2050	74	131	168	216	251	286

Δ = change, GCM = global circulation model, mm = millimeter, RCP = representative concentration pathway.

Notes: The analysis represents changes in the yearly maximum 1-day precipitation (Rx1day) at various return periods, providing predictions of future frequencies of extreme precipitation events. It is based on the third quartile (75th percentile) of ensemble predictions and uses a Gumbel fitting approach to estimate the extreme events. The numbers can be used to inform the design of more climate-resilient urban infrastructure.

ERA5 refers to the 5th generation atmospheric reanalysis of the global climate, covering 1950 to the present.

Source: Asian Development Bank project team and consultant experts, using data from ERA5 (historical) and NASA Earth Exchange climate model projections (RCP45 and RCP85).

2.8 Climate Trends and Risk Analyses: Tbilisi (Tbilisi Province)

SUMMARY (2050)

City-scale risk
- Moderate risk of extreme heat, concentrated in urban center
- Moderate riverine flood risk in many areas of the urban center, roads to north and south

National-scale hazards
- Unlikely to experience water stress problems
- Area unlikely to be exposed to extreme cold events

Changes in climate
- Moderate increases in maximum yearly temperature; increasing frequency and intensity of heat waves
- Moderate increases in maximum 1-day precipitation events may increase flood risk

Extreme precipitation
- The most severe precipitation events predicted by climate model ensemble are of moderate intensity

Figure 2.22: Current Risk Associated with Extreme Heat and Riverine Flooding (Tbilisi)

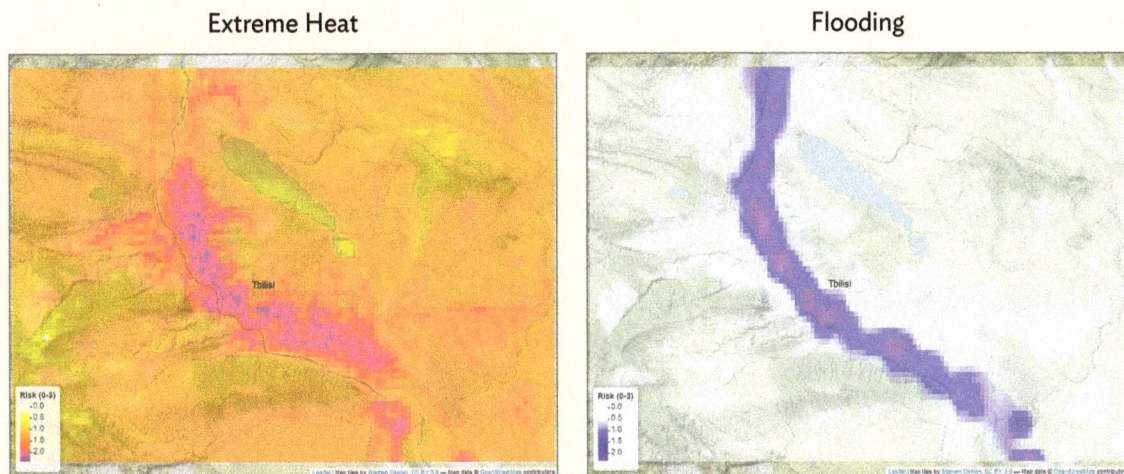

Note: 0 = no risk, 3 = high risk.

Source: Asian Development Bank project team and consultant experts, using data from the United Nations (population density and gross domestic product); OpenStreetMap (vulnerability of road networks, buildings, and points of interest); United Nations Office for Disaster Risk Reduction. 2015. *Global Assessment Report on Disaster Risk Reduction 2015*. Geneva (1 in 100-year flood hazard); and Google Earth Engine (heat anomaly signals).

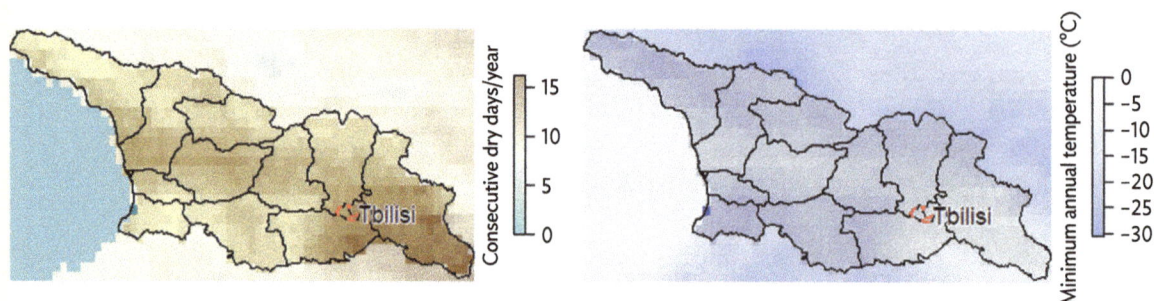

Figure 2.23: Current Hazards Associated with Water Shortage or Drought and Extreme Cold Events (Tbilisi)

Notes: Map shows the spatial distribution of each hazard and the location of the urban area in this context.
    ERA5 refers to the 5th generation atmospheric reanalysis of the global climate, covering 1950 to the present.
Source: Asian Development Bank project team and consultant experts, using data from ERA5 (drought and extreme low temperature).

Table 2.8: Changes in Future Climate under Medium and High Emissions Scenarios (Tbilisi)

Variable	Units [Δ units]	Historic	Δ RCP45 2030	Δ RCP45 2050	Δ RCP85 2030	Δ RCP85 2050
Average climate trends						
Mean Annual Temperature	°C [°C]	12.7	1.3 [0.8, 1.8]	1.9 [1.5, 2.5]	1.4 [0.9, 2]	2.7 [2, 3.4]
Total Annual Precipitation	mm/year [%]	939.9	2.9 [(9.7), 12]	0.7 [(9.2), 13.1]	2.8 [(8.5), 14]	(0.3) [(11.1), 11.6]
Extreme temperature trends						
Maximum Annual Temperature	°C [°C]	31	2 [0.8, 3.1]	2.9 [1.8, 3.9]	2.2 [1.1, 3.3]	3.9 [2.7, 5.3]
Minimum Annual Temperature	°C [°C]	(18.8)	1.1 [(1), 3.5]	1.6 [(0.5), 3.8]	1.6 [(1), 3.8]	2.3 [(0.3), 4.6]
Extreme precipitation trends						
Maximum 1-Day Precipitation	mm/day [%]	44.1	4 [(10.3), 19.8]	3.6 [(12.2), 20.7]	2 [(11.8), 19.9]	4.6 [(11), 22.8]
Drought Period Length	days [days]	19	0.8 [(2.1), 5.3]	1.5 [(1.4), 5.7]	1 [(2.3), 5.7]	3.1 [(0.7), 8.8]

Δ = change, ( ) = negative, mm = millimeter, RCP = representative concentration pathway.

Notes: Numbers in brackets represent median values (25th percentile, 75th percentile) of climate model ensemble predictions.
    ERA5 refers to the 5th generation atmospheric reanalysis of the global climate, covering 1950 to the present.

Source: Asian Development Bank project team and consultant experts, using data from ERA5 (historical) and NASA Earth Exchange climate model projections (RCP45 and RCP85).

Figure 2.24: Return Period Analysis of Extreme Precipitation Events (Tbilisi)

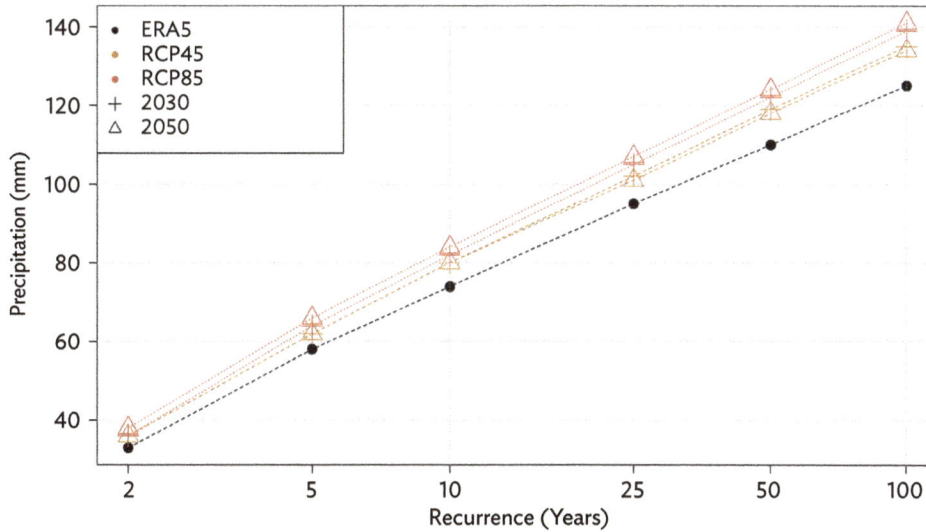

	Return Period					
	2 Years	5 Years	10 Years	25 Years	50 Years	100 Years
Historical daily maximum precipitation (mm)						
ERA5	33	58	74	95	110	125
Future (75th percentile of GCM distribution) (mm)						
RCP45 2030	36	62	80	102	119	135
RCP45 2050	36	62	80	101	118	134
RCP85 2030	36	64	82	105	122	139
RCP85 2050	38	66	84	107	124	141

Δ = change, GCM = global circulation model, mm = millimeter, RCP = representative concentration pathway.

Notes: The analysis represents changes in the yearly maximum 1-day precipitation (Rx1day) at various return periods, providing predictions of future frequencies of extreme precipitation events. It is based on the third quartile (75th percentile) of ensemble predictions and uses a Gumbel fitting approach to estimate the extreme events. The numbers can be used to inform the design of more climate-resilient urban infrastructure.

ERA5 refers to the 5th generation atmospheric reanalysis of the global climate, covering 1950 to the present.

Source: Asian Development Bank project team and consultant experts, using data from ERA5 (historical) and NASA Earth Exchange climate model projections (RCP45 and RCP85).

2.9 Climate Trends and Risk Analyses: Zugdidi (Samegrelo–Zemo Svaneti Province)

SUMMARY (2050)

City-scale risk
- Limited risk of extreme heat events across area, increased risk in urban center
- Moderate riverine flood risk along road networks

National-scale hazards
- Unlikely to experience extreme water stress problems
- Extreme cold events are most likely to affect north of area

Changes in climate
- Large increases in maximum yearly temperature will likely increase frequency and intensity of heat waves
- Moderate increases in maximum 1-day precipitation events may increase flood risk

Extreme precipitation
- The most severe precipitation events predicted by climate model ensemble are of extreme intensity

Figure 2.25: Current Risk Associated with Extreme Heat and Riverine Flooding (Zugdidi)

Extreme Heat   Flooding

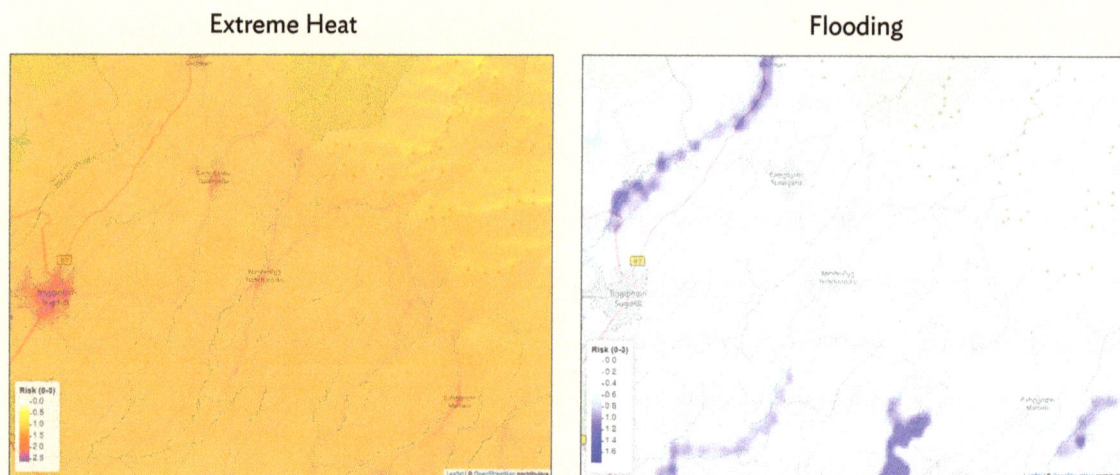

Notes: 0 = no risk, 3 = high risk. The different spelling of Zugdidi in the risk maps is from the OpenStreetMap base map labels.

Source: Asian Development Bank project team and consultant experts, using data from the United Nations (population density and gross domestic product); OpenStreetMap (vulnerability of road networks, buildings, and points of interest); United Nations Office for Disaster Risk Reduction. 2015. *Global Assessment Report on Disaster Risk Reduction 2015*. Geneva (1 in 100-year flood hazard); and Google Earth Engine (heat anomaly signals).

Figure 2.26: Current Hazards Associated with Water Shortage or Drought and Extreme Cold Events (Zugdidi)

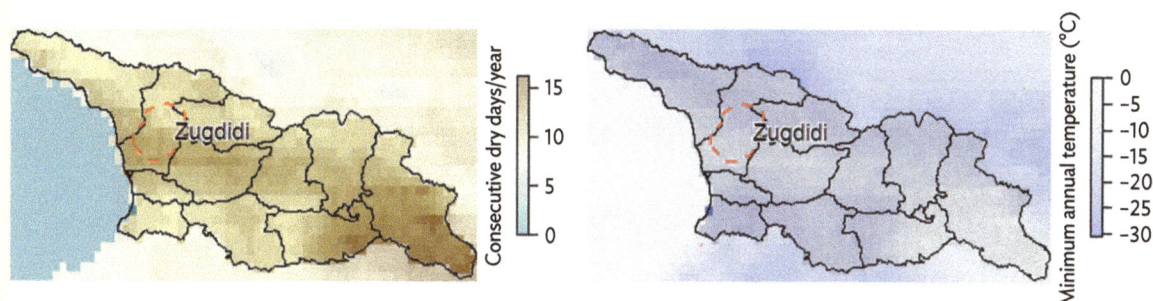

Notes: Map shows the spatial distribution of each hazard and the location of the urban area in this context.
ERA5 refers to the 5th generation atmospheric reanalysis of the global climate, covering 1950 to the present.

Source: Asian Development Bank project team and consultant experts, using data from ERA5 (drought and extreme low temperature).

Table 2.9: Changes in Future Climate under Medium and High Emissions Scenarios (Zugdidi)

Variable	Units [Δ units]	Historic	Δ RCP45 2030	Δ RCP45 2050	Δ RCP85 2030	Δ RCP85 2050
Average climate trends						
Mean Annual Temperature	°C [°C]	12.6	1.3 [0.7, 1.8]	1.9 [1.4, 2.4]	1.4 [0.9, 2]	2.7 [1.9, 3.4]
Total Annual Precipitation	mm/year [%]	1,269	3.6 [(9.6), 13.9]	2.3 [(9.6), 14.4]	3.4 [(8.8), 14.9]	(0.3) [(11.2), 13.2]
Extreme temperature trends						
Maximum Annual Temperature	°C [°C]	29.8	1.9 [0.6, 3]	2.7 [1.5, 3.8]	2.1 [0.9, 3.2]	3.7 [2.4, 5.3]
Minimum Annual Temperature	°C [°C]	(17.7)	1.1 [(1.5), 3.5]	1.6 [(0.6), 4]	1.3 [(1), 3.7]	2.4 [(0.4), 4.7]
Extreme precipitation trends						
Maximum 1-Day Precipitation	mm/day [%]	55.4	7.6 [(10.3), 25.5]	6.8 [(12.6), 25.8]	5.7 [(12.2), 29.7]	6.5 [(10.6), 30.6]
Drought Period Length	days [days]	16.1	0.9 [(2.2), 5.3]	1.1 [(1.7), 5.5]	0.9 [(2.4), 5.2]	3.1 [(0.9), 7.5]

Δ = change, ( ) = negative, mm = millimeter, RCP = representative concentration pathway.

Notes: Numbers in brackets represent median values (25th percentile, 75th percentile) of climate model ensemble predictions.
ERA5 refers to the 5th generation atmospheric reanalysis of the global climate, covering 1950 to the present.

Source: Asian Development Bank project team and consultant experts, using data from ERA5 (historical) and NASA Earth Exchange climate model projections (RCP45 and RCP85).

Figure 2.27: Return Period Analysis of Extreme Precipitation Events (Zugdidi)

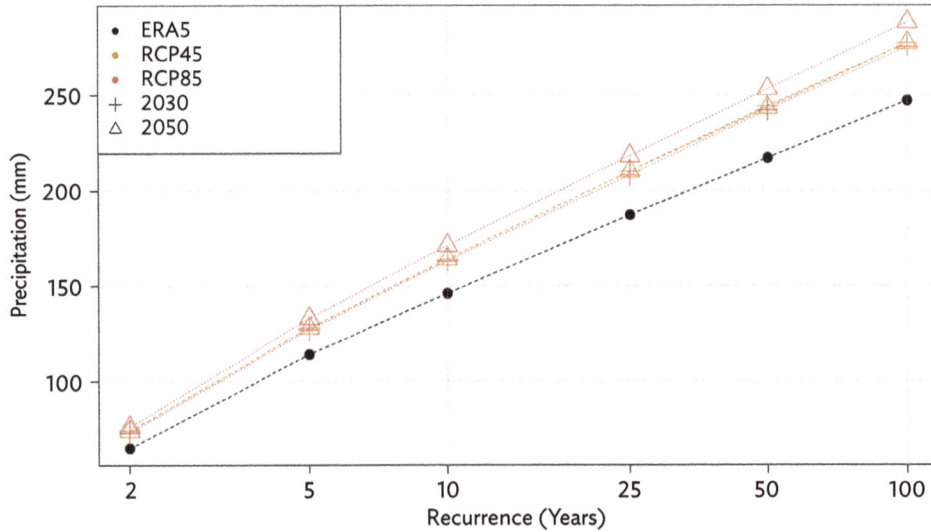

	Return Period					
	2 Years	**5 Years**	**10 Years**	**25 Years**	**50 Years**	**100 Years**
Historical daily maximum precipitation (mm)						
ERA5	65	114	146	187	217	247
Future (75th percentile of GCM distribution) (mm)						
RCP45 2030	74	128	164	210	244	277
RCP45 2050	74	128	164	210	243	277
RCP85 2030	73	127	163	208	242	275
RCP85 2050	76	133	171	218	253	288

Δ = change, GCM = global circulation model, mm = millimeter, RCP = representative concentration pathway.

Notes: The analysis represents changes in the yearly maximum 1-day precipitation (Rx1day) at various return periods, providing predictions of future frequencies of extreme precipitation events. It is based on the third quartile (75th percentile) of ensemble predictions and uses a Gumbel fitting approach to estimate the extreme events. The numbers can be used to inform the design of more climate-resilient urban infrastructure.

ERA5 refers to the 5th generation atmospheric reanalysis of the global climate, covering 1950 to the present.

Source: Asian Development Bank project team and consultant experts, using data from ERA5 (historical) and NASA Earth Exchange climate model projections (RCP45 and RCP85).

2.10 Options for Mainstreaming Climate Change in Urban Planning

Key Considerations in Selected Subsectors

Adaptation starts at the planning stage. Taking climate change risks into account in both land-use planning and siting of infrastructure is of paramount importance, as is answering questions such as "Which infrastructure projects are needed to enhance urban climate resilience?" And "Is this project appropriate within the urban risk context?"

Table 2.10 provides some specific measures that may be considered in the planning process at the national level. The focus of this table is on key subsectors that may be affected by climate change and correspond to the priority areas of ADB investment. Although relevant, health and energy are beyond the scope of this profile.

Table 2.10: Planning Considerations for Selected Urban Subsectors

Projected Climate Change	Relevance to Area (Low/Medium/High)[a]	Potential Impacts on Infrastructure	Possible Planning Considerations and/or Actions
Transport Infrastructure			
Small to moderate increases in precipitation intensity and maximum 1-day precipitation events	**High** High precipitation in the country will likely cause problems along large river channels. The northeastern provinces, with steep topography, and coastal provinces, with intense precipitation, are especially at risk.	Increased precipitation potentially leading to increased damage to roads and transport infrastructure due to floods, mudslides, landslides, and avalanches	• Take account of flooding risks in decisions regarding the siting of roads and rails and related transport infrastructure • Incorporate blue and green spaces in planning to cope with excess water • Encourage mixed-use, vertical, and compact development as opposed to urban sprawl to reduce dependence on car-centric lifestyles
Moderate increase in maximum temperatures and frequency of heat waves	**Medium** Georgia does not experience extreme heat regularly. Urban centers are at risk of urban heat island effect.	Intense heat waves and increased temperatures potentially affecting transport infrastructure and requiring more frequent repairs, as well as affecting users	Encourage the use of nature-based solutions,[b] such as tree planting, creation of urban water bodies, and green roofs to reduce the urban heat island effect
Moderate increase in minimum yearly temperatures, considerable decrease in frost days	**Medium** Most likely to be a consideration in higher elevation areas to north and south.	Increases in minimum temperatures potentially leading to a decrease in frost- and ice-related damage to infrastructure	No adaptation needed to address climate change risks, possibly a gain from climate change to be realized

continued on next page

Table 2.10 *continued*

Projected Climate Change	Relevance to Area (Low/Medium/High)[a]	Potential Impacts on Infrastructure	Possible Planning Considerations and/or Actions
Buildings			
Small to moderate increases in precipitation intensity, maximum 1-day precipitation events	**High** High precipitation will likely cause problems along large river channels. Northeastern provinces, with steep topography, and coastal provinces, with intense precipitation, are especially vulnerable.	Increased precipitation potentially leading to increased damage to buildings due to floods, mudslides, landslides, and avalanches	• Climate-informed land-use planning (e.g., siting of buildings) • Climate-resilient building codes • Upgrading of existing surface water management and drainage infrastructure for increased intensity precipitation events • Incorporation of SUDS features in the planning process • Early warning systems
Moderate increase in maximum temperatures and frequency of heat waves	**Medium** Georgia does not regularly experience extreme heat; however, extreme heat may be an issue in large urban centers.	Intense heat waves and increased temperatures potentially affecting buildings and users	• Building guidelines to improve temperature regulation in buildings and encourage the use of heat-resistant materials • Green-blue infrastructure such as urban greenspace, water features, green roofs, and shading trees
Moderate increase in minimum yearly temperatures, considerable decrease in frost days	**Medium** This is most likely to be an issue in higher elevation areas to the north and south.	Increases in minimum temperatures potentially leading to a decrease in frost- and ice-related damage to buildings	No adaptation needed to address climate change risks, possibly a gain from climate change to be realized
Sanitation, Sewerage, and Water Supply			
Moderate increases in precipitation intensity, maximum 1-day precipitation events	**High** This could lead to high precipitation nationwide, although it is likely to be more of an issue in northeastern and coastal areas with high precipitation in expansive urban areas.	Increased extreme precipitation events may exceed urban water cycle capacity	• Enhance land-use planning focusing on increasing percentage of permeable and semipermeable greenspace and creating water storage and retention in urban areas[c] • Upgrade capacity of sewerage networks • Shift from combined sewerage and drainage networks to separate systems • Incorporate SUDSs in drainage planning • Develop and implement climate-resilient drainage and wastewater management plans
Small increase in drought length, decrease or small increase in total precipitation	**Low** Georgia is not especially water stressed, and therefore may be less prepared for increases in intensity and frequency of drought.	Increased intensity of droughts may cause water shortages	• Increased water efficiency (loss reduction) in infrastructure • Demand management measures[d] • Diversification of water supply, water recycling, and use of alternative water resources[e] • Implementation of drought management and early warning strategies

continued on next page

Table 2.10 *continued*

Projected Climate Change	Relevance to Area (Low/Medium/High)[a]	Potential Impacts on Infrastructure	Possible Planning Considerations and/or Actions
Solid Waste			
Moderate increase in maximum annual temperatures.	Medium Most likely to be an issue in higher elevation areas to the north and south where the climate may become milder.	Increased temperature may require an improvement of the waste management system to cope with potentially increased risks of pathogenic germs to health	• 3Rs (reduce, reuse, and recycling) awareness raising and waste minimization campaigns • Upgrading of landfill sites to avoid mobilization of pollutants and reduce methane emissions

SUDS = sustainable urban drainage system.

[a] Relevance ratings are determined by expert judgment based on relevant datasets presented in the climate risk profiles.

[b] More guidance may be obtained from J. Matthews and E. O. Dela Cruz. 2022. *Integrating Nature-Based Solutions for Climate Change Adaptation and Disaster Risk Management: A Practitioner's Guide*. Manila: ADB.

[c] See the "sponge city" concept piloted in several cities in the People's Republic of China with support from ADB. ADB. 2017. Piloting "Sponge Cities" in the People's Republic of China. Project result/case study. 13 January.

[d] This includes a variety of measures such as tariffs, pricing, user controls, awareness raising, and smart network monitoring.

[e] There exist technologies that can use brackish water or wastewater as inputs and produce a combination of food (aquaculture products, vegetables, animal feed) and clean water. Applicability for Georgia would need to be assessed. The advantage of such technology is that it involves an ecosystem-based approach in line with Georgia's nationally determined contribution.

Source: Asian Development Bank project team.

Considerations on Enabling Environment, Local Government Planning, and Operation and Maintenance

Prompt action on other general considerations relating to planning and O&M can enhance urban climate resiliency building in Georgia. Some of these considerations are listed below.

Enabling environment for climate resilience planning

The central government can consider the following measures:

- Ensure that local governments and stakeholders are equipped with adequate data, information, and skills that will help them respond to the impacts of climate change. This could be in the form of data portals and knowledge-sharing workshops.
- Ensure that cities coping with climate change have sufficient access to finance, for example, by providing access to international climate finance through applications by the central government to financing sources such as the Green Climate Fund.
- Ensure that individuals and communities affected by climate change-related hazards can recover and rebuild as quickly as possible via access to insurance and national government support programs.
- Develop building codes and standards for infrastructure that consider changes in climate, such as new flood return periods.
- Introduce and institutionalize risk-based land use and open space planning. Introduce blue-green resilience networks and nature-based solutions as a first step in spatial planning.
- Initiate and sustain benchmarking and monitoring of efforts across cities and local government jurisdictions, facilitating knowledge transfer between these parties.

Local government planning

Local governments may wish to consider the measures below.

- Take account of how expected climate change interacts with the cities' development visions and how expected climate change may impact the relative viability of investments. This is especially relevant to assess the performance of built assets over their respective project life cycles.
- Develop climate hazard maps to guide urban development, e.g., to integrate flood risks into urban spatial planning. This requires local-scale, higher-resolution modeling to better map the influence on hazards of a full envelope of likely changes in climate.
- Ensure that individuals and communities at risk to climate-related hazards are aware of the risks they are exposed to and how these may change in the future. This could be achieved via community outreach and digital applications.
- Climate hazard information should be factored into the design and implementation of development regulation instruments, such as zoning, land subdivision, and building codes. This will help reduce climate change vulnerability and avoid the expansion of development to high-risk areas.
- Adopt, implement, and enforce building codes and standards for infrastructure that consider changes in climate, such as new flood return periods.
- Promote the development of early warning systems and climate change-related disaster response strategies (often as part of a more comprehensive disaster response strategy).
- Initiate community-level education programs for disaster preparedness. These should focus on preparing communities for situations in which authorities and emergency services are unable to access affected areas to provide critical assistance in the aftermath of a disaster.
- Undertake institutional strengthening for climate action through reform of responsibilities and creation of a high-level climate change office under the governor and mayor and cross-departmental working groups.

Operation and maintenance

Adequate O&M is as important as up-front capital investments to ensure resilience of infrastructure and other physical assets to climate risk. Key considerations relating to O&M include the following:

- Ensure that risk-informed O&M is considered from the earliest stages of planning and design for new infrastructure projects.
- Update existing O&M plans to reflect changes in precipitation and temperature, which may necessitate more frequent maintenance or changes in operational practices.
- Create backup emergency infrastructure in case of failure in key infrastructure, e.g., the maintenance of emergency generators in case of power failure.
- Ensure regular inspection and maintenance of infrastructure relating to hazard protection, e.g., flood protection structures.
- Implement smart monitoring strategies and the Internet of Things, which collect, centralize, and review data relating to hydrometeorology and key infrastructure.
- Implement risk-informed preventive maintenance, which may be a highly feasible and cost-effective approach for ensuring overall network resilience.
- Prioritize the O&M of telecommunication networks, which play a critical role in disaster response efforts.

2.11 Infrastructure Design Considerations

Table 2.11 provides some key considerations for the design and/or upgrading of urban infrastructure assets to enhance climate resilience based on expert judgment of climate model ensemble outputs, including possible adaptation measures. As with Table 2.10, the focus of this table is on key urban subsectors that may be affected by climate change and correspond to priority areas of ADB investment. Health and energy, while potentially relevant, are beyond the scope of this profile.

Table 2.11: Design Considerations for Urban Infrastructure in Selected Cities

Projected Climate Change	Relevance to Area (Low / Medium / High)								Potential Impact on Infrastructure	Possible Adaptation Measures
	Batumi	Gori	Kutaisi	Mestia-Lentekhi	Northern Kakheti	Poti	Tbilisi	Zugdidi	Batumi, Gori, Kutaisi, Mestia-Lentekhi, Northern Kakheti, Poti, Tbilisi, Zugdidi	Batumi, Gori, Kutaisi, Mestia-Lentekhi, Northern Kakheti, Poti, Tbilisi, Zugdidi
Transport Infrastructure										
Moderate increases in precipitation intensity, maximum 1-day precipitation events	Medium. Riverine flood risk along road networks and west of urban center	High. Riverine flood risk along road networks and urban center, risk of landslide in area, pluvial flood risks also likely	High. Riverine flood risk along road networks and urban center, pluvial flood risks also likely	High. Riverine flood risk along road networks, risk of landslide in north of area, flash flood risks also likely	Medium. Riverine flood risk along road networks, risk of landslide in north of area	High. Riverine flood risk along road networks and urban area to north of center, pluvial and coastal flood risks also likely	High. Riverine flood risk throughout city center and road networks to north and south	High. Riverine flood risk along road networks, risk of landslide in north of area, pluvial flood risks also likely	Increased precipitation potentially leading to increased damage to roads and transport infrastructure due to floods, mudslides, landslides, and avalanches	• Enhance drainage • Reinforce vulnerable structures • Utilize permeable road and pavements • Increase the height and setback of flood defenses and dikes
Small increase in maximum temperatures and frequency of heat waves	Medium. Problematic in urban center	Medium. Risk concentrated in large urban center	Medium. Problematic in urban center, along road networks	Low. Problematic in urban center, along road networks	Medium. Problematic in urban center, along road networks	Medium. Problematic in urban center	Medium. Risk concentrated in large urban center	Medium. Problematic in urban center, along road networks	Intense heat waves and increased temperatures potentially affecting transport infrastructure and requiring more frequent repairs, as well as affecting users	• Use road construction materials that are more resistant to heat[a] • Use road construction materials with self-healing properties[b] • Plant trees along roadsides • Enhance ventilation and cooling for public transport systems

continued on next page

Table 2.11 *continued*

| Projected Climate Change | Relevance to Area (Low / Medium / High) | | | | | | | | Potential Impact on Infrastructure | Possible Adaptation Measures |
	Batumi	Gori	Kutaisi	Mestia-Lentekhi	Northern Kakheti	Poti	Tbilisi	Zugdidi	Batumi, Gori, Kutaisi, Mestia-Lentekhi, Northern Kakheti, Poti, Tbilisi, Zugdidi	
Moderate increase in minimum yearly temperature, considerable decrease in frost days	Low — Limited extreme cold events in area	Medium — Likely more common in urban center	Medium — Likely more common in urban center	Medium — Most applicable along road networks	Medium — Likely more common in urban center	Low — Limited extreme cold events in area	Medium — Extreme low temperatures will become less frequent, even less so in warm city center	Medium — Likely more common in urban center	Increases in minimum temperatures potentially leading to a decrease in frost- and ice-related damage to infrastructure	No adaptation needed to address climate change risks, possibly a gain from climate change to be realized
Buildings										
Moderate increases in precipitation intensity, maximum 1-day precipitation events	High — Riverine flood risk in urban area to south of center, pluvial and coastal flood risks also likely	High — Riverine flood risk in urban center, risk of landslide in area, pluvial flood risks also likely	High — Riverine flood risk in urban center, pluvial flood risks also likely	High — Risk of landslide in north of area, flash flood risks also likely	Medium — May be some risk of flash flooding, risk of landslide in north of area	High — Riverine flood risk in urban area to north of center, pluvial and coastal flood risks also likely	High — Riverine flood risk throughout the city center, some risk of pluvial flooding	High — Likely pluvial flood risk in urban center, risk of landslide in north of area	Increased precipitation potentially leading to increased damage to buildings due to floods, mudslides, landslides, and avalanches	• Enhanced drainage infrastructure to cope with increased intensity precipitation events • SUDS features, e.g., retention basins, bioswales • Daylighting of streams and river and/or floodplain restoration • Protective infrastructure such as flood barriers, slope stabilization measures, and dams • Bracing technologies against strong winds

continued on next page

Table 2.11 *continued*

Projected Climate Change	Relevance to Area (Low / Medium / High)								Potential Impact on Infrastructure	Possible Adaptation Measures Batumi, Gori, Kutaisi, Mestia-Lentekhi, Northern Kakheti, Poti, Tbilisi, Zugdidi
	Batumi	Gori	Kutaisi	Mestia-Lentekhi	Northern Kakheti	Poti	Tbilisi	Zugdidi		
Moderate increase in maximum temperatures and frequency of heat waves	Medium — Problematic in urban center	Medium — Risk concentrated in large urban center	Medium — Most pertinent in urban center	Low — Increases in extreme temperatures may be offset by low urban density	Medium — Increases in extreme temperatures may be offset by low urban density	Medium — Problematic in urban center	Medium — Risk concentrated in large urban center	Medium — Increases in extreme temperatures may be offset by low urban density	Intense heat waves and increased temperatures potentially affecting buildings and users	• White roofs • Green roofs and shading trees • Airtight and double-glazed glass windows and doors • Increased thermal mass of buildings • Use of heat-reflective materials to minimize solar heat gain • Provision of ventilation • Efficient cooling
Moderate increase in minimum yearly temperatures, considerable decrease in frost days	Low — Limited extreme cold events in area	Medium — Likely more common in urban center	High — Risk of pluvial flooding if drainage networks not upgraded	Medium — Most applicable along road networks	Medium — Likely more common in urban center	Low — Limited extreme cold events in area	Medium — Extreme low temperatures will be less frequent, even less so in warm city center	Medium — Likely more common in urban center	Increases in minimum temperatures potentially leading to a decrease in frost- and ice-related damages to buildings	No adaptation needed to address climate change risks, possibly a gain from climate change to be realized

continued on next page

Table 2.11 *continued*

Projected Climate Change	Relevance to Area (Low / Medium / High)								Potential Impact on Infrastructure	Possible Adaptation Measures Batumi, Gori, Kutaisi, Mestia-Lentekhi, Northern Kakheti, Poti, Tbilisi, Zugdidi
	Batumi	Gori	Kutaisi	Mestia-Lentekhi	Northern Kakheti	Poti	Tbilisi	Zugdidi		
Sanitation, Sewerage, and Water Supply										
Moderate increases in precipitation intensity, maximum 1-day precipitation events	High Risk of pluvial flooding if drainage networks not upgraded	High Risk of pluvial flooding if drainage networks not upgraded	High Risk of pluvial flooding if drainage networks not upgraded	High Risk of pluvial flooding if drainage networks not upgraded	Medium Risk of pluvial flooding if drainage networks not upgraded	High Risk of pluvial flooding if drainage networks not upgraded	High May be complicated by complexities due to size of city	High Risk of pluvial flooding if drainage networks not upgraded	Increased extreme precipitation events may exceed urban water cycle capacity	• Upgrade drainage and/or sewerage assets to increase capacity for high-intensity precipitation events • Install SUDSs e.g., bioswales, retention basins • Consider separating stormwater and wastewater • Install treatment wetlands to support wastewater treatment infrastructure
Small increase in drought length, increase in total precipitation	Low Limited drought problems in area	Low Limited drought problems in area	Low Limited drought problems in area	Low Limited drought problems in area	Low Limited drought problems in area	Low Limited drought problems in area	Low High total precipitation in area, may be aggravated by complexities due to size of city	Low Limited drought problems in area	Potentially increased intensity of droughts may cause water shortages	• Diversification of water source: groundwater and surface water • Water reuse and recycling • Rainwater harvesting • Wastewater reuse for agricultural irrigation and industrial purposes

continued on next page

Table 2.11 *continued*

Projected Climate Change	Relevance to Area (Low / Medium / High)								Potential Impact on Infrastructure	Possible Adaptation Measures
	Batumi	Gori	Kutaisi	Mestia-Lentekhi	Northern Kakheti	Poti	Tbilisi	Zugdidi	Batumi, Gori, Kutaisi, Mestia-Lentekhi, Northern Kakheti, Poti, Tbilisi, Zugdidi	
Solid Waste										
Moderate increases in maximum annual temperatures	Medium Problematic in urban center	Medium May be problematic in urban center	Medium May be problematic in urban center	Medium May be problematic in urban center	Medium May be problematic in urban center	Medium May be problematic in urban center	Medium May be problematic in urban center	Medium May be problematic in urban center	Increased temperature may require an improvement of the waste management system to cope with potentially increased risks of pathogenic germs to health	• Enhance waste collection, storage, and processing as appropriate • Waste collection and treatment could combine recycling and reuse, anaerobic digestion, and incineration

SUDS = sustainable urban drainage system.

a Examples include warm-mix asphalt and engineered cementitious composites.

b Materials with self-healing properties are materials that automatically fill cracks without human intervention. Different materials (including concretes based on pozzolanic materials, concretes based on cements with added bacteria, and concrete with special coatings) can exhibit this behavior and may be used for road and bridge construction.

Source: Asian Development Bank project team.

3. Uzbekistan

3.1 Climate Trends and Risk Analyses: National Level

SUMMARY (2050)

Averages
- Increase in average yearly temperature predicted by all climate models
- No clear signal in predictions for precipitation changes at the national level

Extremes
- Increases in maximum yearly temperature and number of days where a temperature of more than 35 degrees Celsius suggests increasing frequency and intensity of heat waves
- Moderate increases in maximum 1-day precipitation events may lead to increased flood risk

Seasonality
- Increases in average temperatures for all months
- Little shift in the seasonality of precipitation

Spatial distribution
- Eastern provinces likely to experience greatest increases in temperature, western provinces greatest increases in extreme heat events
- Eastern provinces likely to experience greatest increases in precipitation and extreme rainfall events

Bibi Khanym Mosque in Samarkand, Uzbekistan (photo by Eric Sales/ADB).

Figure 3.1: Past and Future Changes in Temperature and Precipitation under Medium and High Emissions Scenarios (Uzbekistan)

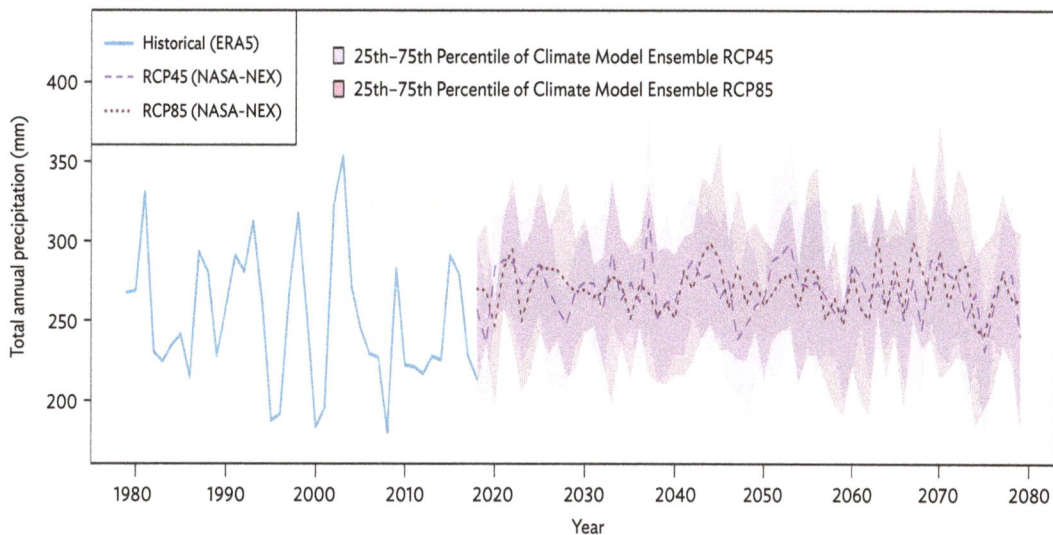

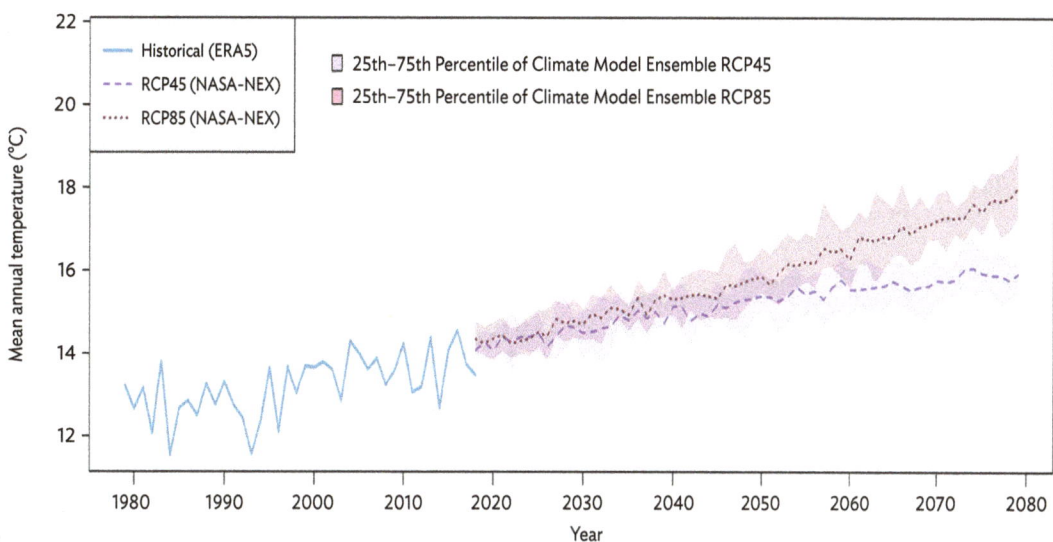

mm = millimeter, NASA-NEX = NASA Earth Exchange, RCP = representative concentration pathway.

Notes: Shaded areas indicate the 25th and 75th percentiles of climate model ensemble predictions, reflecting the full spread of model predictions. ERA5 refers to the 5th generation atmospheric reanalysis of the global climate, covering 1950 to the present.

Source: Asian Development Bank project team and consultant experts, using data from ERA5 (historical) and NASA-NEX climate model projections (RCP45 and RCP85).

Figure 3.2: Per-Province Changes in Temperature and Precipitation under a Medium Emissions Scenario (Uzbekistan)

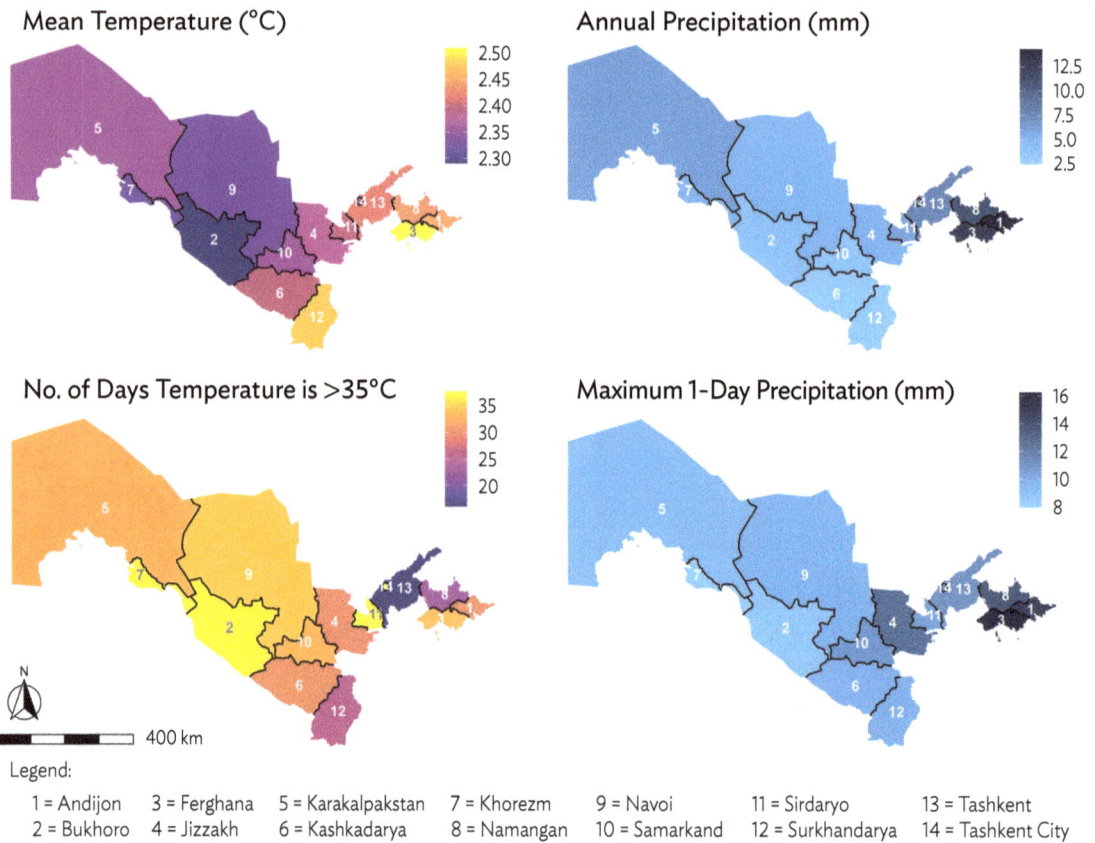

Mean Temperature (°C)

Annual Precipitation (mm)

No. of Days Temperature is >35°C

Maximum 1-Day Precipitation (mm)

400 km

Legend:
1 = Andijon	3 = Ferghana	5 = Karakalpakstan	7 = Khorezm	9 = Navoi	11 = Sirdaryo	13 = Tashkent
2 = Bukhoro	4 = Jizzakh	6 = Kashkadarya	8 = Namangan	10 = Samarkand	12 = Surkhandarya	14 = Tashkent City

> = greater than, mm = millimeter, RCP = representative concentration pathway.

Notes: Spatial trends represent changes from the historical (1990) to the future (2050) RCP45 scenario.
ERA5 refers to the 5th generation atmospheric reanalysis of the global climate, covering 1950 to the present.

Source: Asian Development Bank project team and consultant experts, using data from ERA5 and NASA Earth Exchange.

A warm day in Khiva, an old town along the Silk Road in Uzbekistan (photo by Relisa Granovskaya/ADB).

Table 3.1: Summary of National-Level Changes in Future Climate under Medium and High Emissions Scenarios (Uzbekistan)

Variable	Units [Δ units]	Historic	Δ RCP45 2030	Δ RCP45 2050	Δ RCP85 2030	Δ RCP85 2050
Average climate trends						
Mean Annual Temperature	°C [°C]	13.7	**1.4** [0.2, 2.4]	**2.1** [1, 3.2]	**1.5** [0.5, 2.6]	**2.7** [1.2, 3.9]
Total Annual Precipitation	mm/day [%]	273.5	**3.6** [(25.2), 38.9]	**1.8** [(28.2), 39.3]	**(0.2)** [(29.8), 38]	**1.5** [(30.5), 38.9]
Extreme temperature trends						
Maximum Annual Temperature	°C [°C]	39.3	**1.6** [0.3, 3.1]	**2.3** [0.8, 4]	**1.8** [0.4, 3.5]	**3** [1.5, 4.8]
Minimum Annual Temperature	°C [°C]	(17.2)	**1.7** [(3.8), 6.2]	**2.4** [(2.9), 6.3]	**2.1** [(3.7), 6]	**3.3** [(2.2), 7]
Extreme precipitation trends						
Maximum 1-Day Precipitation	mm/day [%]	17.6	**3.2** [(25), 41.7]	**7.7** [(23.1), 41.3]	**3.5** [(27.7), 46.3]	**7.1** [(22.3), 48.2]
Drought Period Length	days [days]	151.7	**(0.2)** [(12.9), 18.5]	**0.4** [(12.2), 19.5]	**1.7** [(12.8), 19.6]	**2.9** [(11.9), 27.9]

Δ = change, ( ) = negative, mm = millimeter, RCP = representative concentration pathway.

Notes: Numbers in brackets represent median values (25th percentile, 75th percentile) of climate model ensemble predictions.
ERA5 refers to the 5th generation atmospheric reanalysis of the global climate, covering 1950 to the present.

Source: Asian Development Bank project team and consultant experts, using data from ERA5 (historical) and NASA Earth Exchange climate model projections (RCP45 and RCP85).

The operation and maintenance of buildings in Tashkent and other urban centers in Uzbekistan should consider the projected more frequent and intense heat waves from an energy efficiency perspective (photo by Relisa Granovskaya/ADB).

Figure 3.3: Seasonal Changes in Temperature and Precipitation, Historical and Future Time Horizons (Uzbekistan)

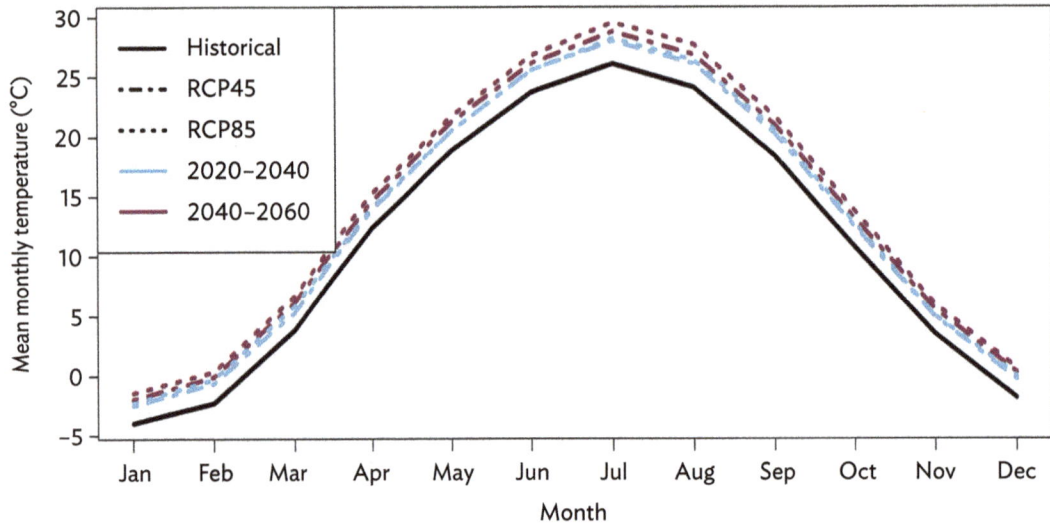

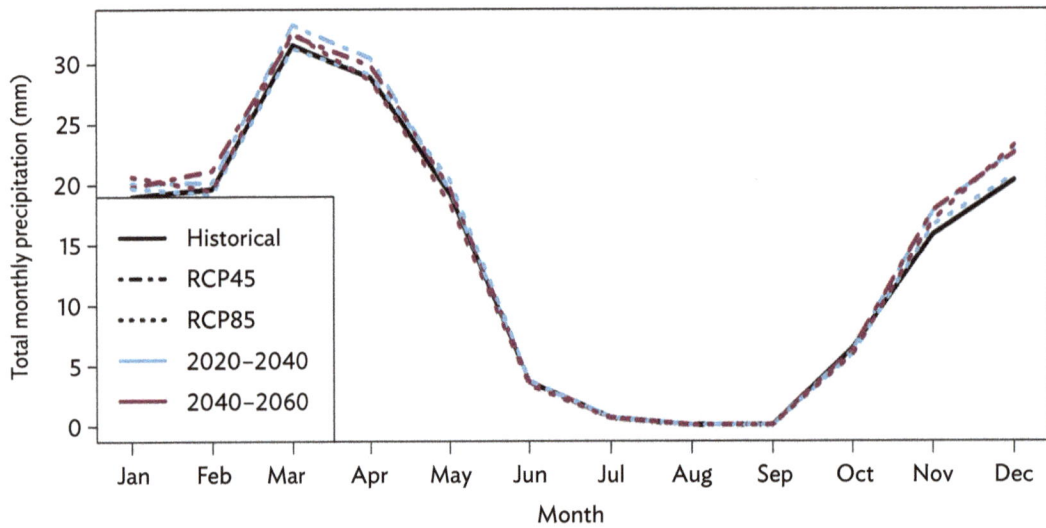

mm = millimeter, RCP = representative concentration pathway.

Notes: Historical data represent changes in total monthly precipitation in 1996–2015.
    ERA5 refers to the 5th generation atmospheric reanalysis of the global climate, covering 1950 to the present.

Source: Asian Development Bank project team and consultant experts, using data from ERA5 (historical) and NASA Earth Exchange climate model projections (RCP45 and RCP85).

3.2 Climate Trends and Risk Analyses: Djizzak (Jizzakh Province)

SUMMARY (2050)

City-scale risk
- High risk of extreme heat, concentrated in urban areas
- Flooding may be an issue, with areas to west and east of urban center exposed to risk

National-scale hazards
- Likely to experience water stress problems
- Area likely frequently exposed to extreme cold events

Changes in climate
- Moderate increases in maximum yearly temperature increasing frequency and intensity of heat waves
- Large increases in maximum 1-day precipitation events may increase flood risk

Extreme precipitation
- The most severe precipitation events predicted by climate model ensemble are of moderate intensity

Figure 3.4: Current Risk Associated with Extreme Heat and Riverine Flooding (Djizzak)

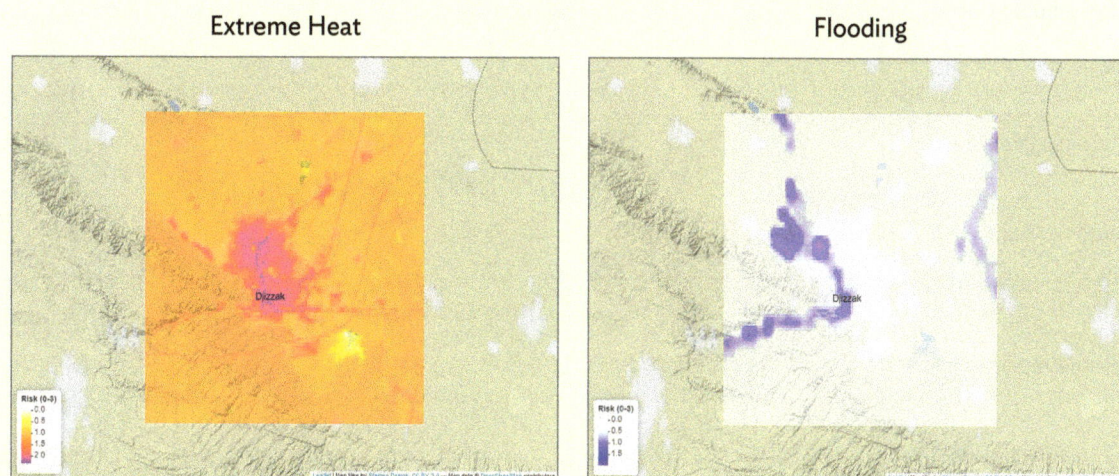

Note: 0 = no risk, 3 = high risk.

Source: Asian Development Bank project team and consultant experts, using data from the United Nations (population density and gross domestic product); OpenStreetMap (vulnerability of road networks, buildings, and points of interest); United Nations Office for Disaster Risk Reduction. 2015. *Global Assessment Report on Disaster Risk Reduction 2015*. Geneva (1 in 100-year flood hazard); and Google Earth Engine (heat anomaly signals).

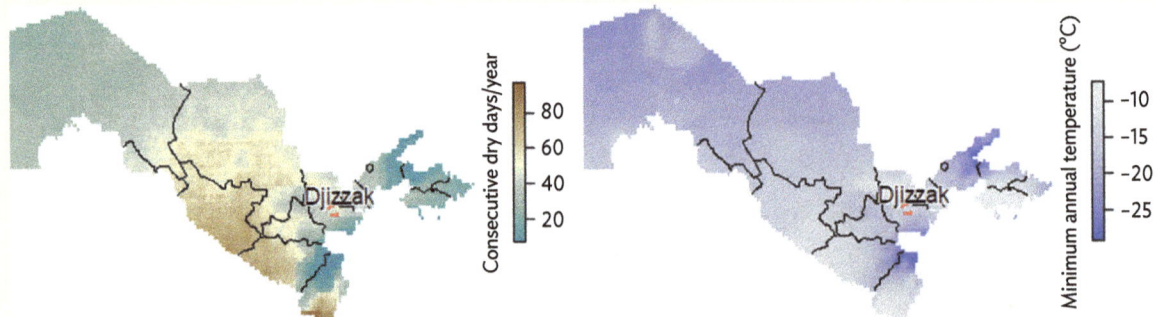

Figure 3.5: Current Hazards Associated with Water Shortage or Drought and Extreme Cold Events (Djizzak)

.Notes: Map shows the spatial distribution of each hazard and the location of the urban area in this context.
ERA5 refers to the 5th generation atmospheric reanalysis of the global climate, covering 1950 to the present.
Source: Asian Development Bank project team and consultant experts, using data from ERA5 (drought and extreme low temperature).

Table 3.2: Changes in Future Climate under Medium and High Emissions Scenarios (Djizzak)

Variable	Units [Δ units]	Historic	Δ RCP45 2030	Δ RCP45 2050	Δ RCP85 2030	Δ RCP85 2050
Average climate trends						
Mean Annual Temperature	°C [°C]	19.3	1.4 [0.8, 1.9]	2 [1.5, 2.7]	1.5 [1, 2.1]	2.6 [1.9, 3.5]
Total Annual Precipitation	mm/year [%]	369.4	3 [(12.4), 23.4]	2 [(15.8), 22.9]	(1.0) [(17.5), 18.7]	1 [(16.8), 22.7]
Extreme temperature trends						
Maximum Annual Temperature	°C [°C]	38	1.5 [0.7, 2.5]	2.4 [1.4, 3.5]	1.9 [0.9, 3]	3.1 [2.2, 4.3]
Minimum Annual Temperature	°C [°C]	(13.9)	1.8 [(0.9), 4.1]	2.2 [(0.5), 4.6]	1.9 [(0.6), 4.5]	3 [0.5, 5.2]
Extreme precipitation trends						
Maximum 1-Day Precipitation	mm/day [%]	29.6	6.3 [(16.8), 32]	11.8 [(14.8), 38.5]	7.1 [(17.8), 35.2]	13.4 [(10.5), 41.2]
Drought Period Length	days [days]	129.8	3.6 [(6.1), 14.4]	2.4 [(6.5), 11.6]	3.3 [(8.4), 14.4]	5.7 [(3.8), 16.6]

Δ = change, ( ) = negative, mm = millimeter, RCP = representative concentration pathway.

Notes: Numbers in brackets represent median values (25th percentile, 75th percentile) of climate model ensemble predictions.
ERA5 refers to the 5th generation atmospheric reanalysis of the global climate, covering 1950 to the present.

Source: Asian Development Bank project team and consultant experts, using data from ERA5 (historical) and NASA Earth Exchange climate model projections (RCP45 and RCP85).

Figure 3.6: Return Period Analysis of Extreme Precipitation Events (Djizzak)

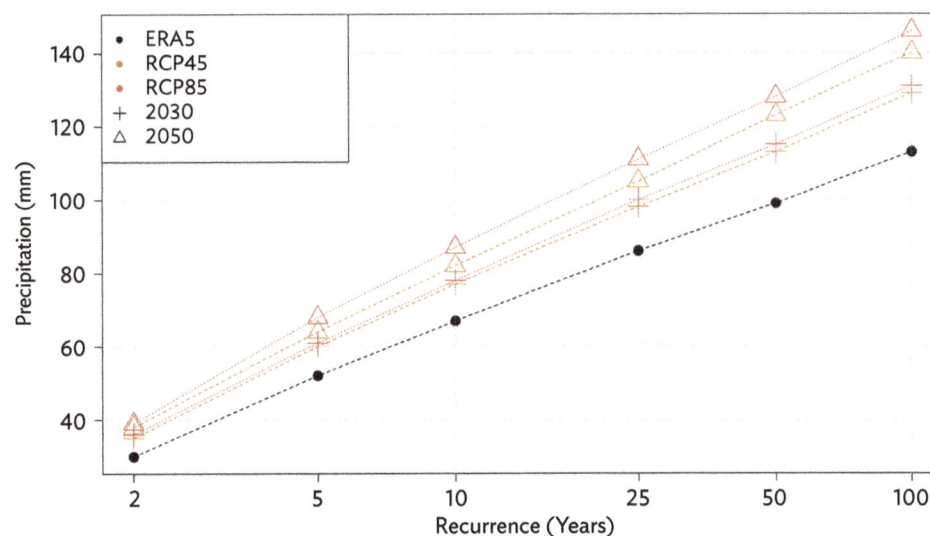

	Return Period					
	2 Years	5 Years	10 Years	25 Years	50 Years	100 Years
Historical daily maximum precipitation (mm)						
ERA5	30	52	67	86	99	113
Future (75th percentile of GCM distribution) (mm)						
RCP45 2030	35	60	77	98	113	129
RCP45 2050	38	64	82	105	123	140
RCP85 2030	36	61	78	100	115	131
RCP85 2050	39	68	87	111	128	146

Δ = change, GCM = global circulation model, mm = millimeter, RCP = representative concentration pathway.

Notes: The analysis represents changes in the yearly maximum 1-day precipitation (Rx1day) at various return periods, providing predictions of future frequencies of extreme precipitation events. It is based on the third quartile (75th percentile) of ensemble predictions and uses a Gumbel fitting approach to estimate the extreme events. The numbers can be used to inform the design of more climate-resilient urban infrastructure.

ERA5 refers to the 5th generation atmospheric reanalysis of the global climate, covering 1950 to the present.

Source: Asian Development Bank project team and consultant experts, using data from ERA5 (historical) and NASA Earth Exchange climate model projections (RCP45 and RCP85).

3.3 Climate Trends and Risk Analyses: Khiva (Khorezm Province)

SUMMARY (2050)

City-scale risk
- High risk of extreme heat events in urban areas
- Low risk of flooding in urban areas

National-scale hazards
- Likely to experience extreme water scarcity issues
- Area likely to be frequently exposed to extreme cold events

Changes in climate
- Moderate increase in maximum yearly temperature increasing frequency and intensity of heat waves
- Large increase in total precipitation, moderate increases in maximum 1-day precipitation events may increase flood risk

Extreme precipitation
- The most severe precipitation events predicted by climate model ensemble are of low intensity

Figure 3.7: Current Risk Associated with Extreme Heat and Riverine Flooding (Khiva)

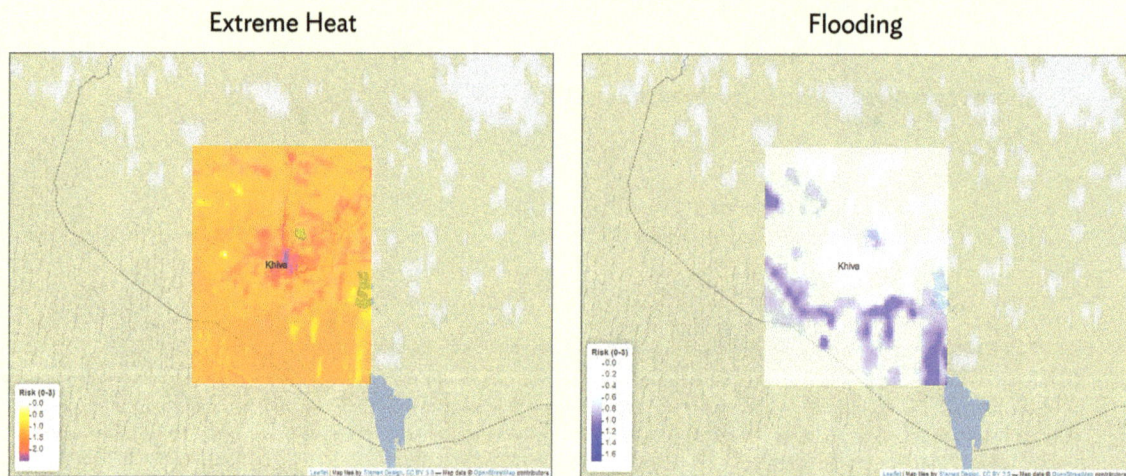

Note: 0 = no risk, 3 = high risk.

Source: Asian Development Bank project team and consultant experts, using data from the United Nations (population density and gross domestic product); OpenStreetMap (vulnerability of road networks, buildings, and points of interest); United Nations Office for Disaster Risk Reduction. 2015. *Global Assessment Report on Disaster Risk Reduction 2015*. Geneva (1 in 100-year flood hazard); and Google Earth Engine (heat anomaly signals).

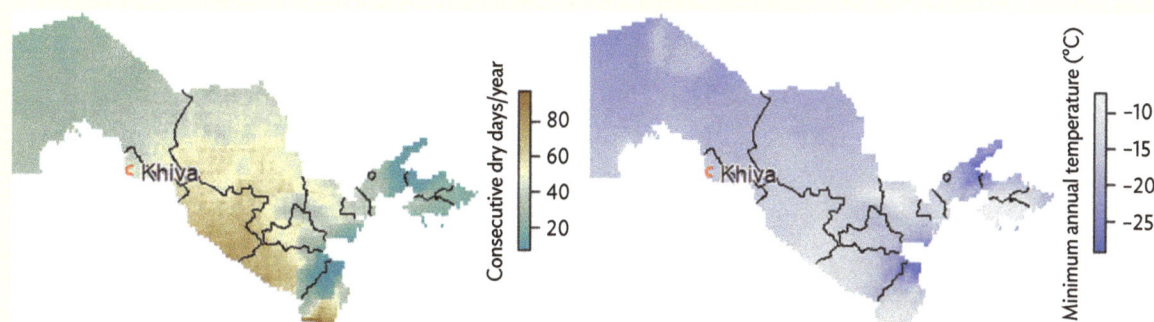

Figure 3.8: Current Hazards Associated with Water Shortage or Drought and Extreme Cold Events (Khiva)

Notes: Map shows the spatial distribution of each hazard and the location of the urban area in this context.
ERA5 refers to the 5th generation atmospheric reanalysis of the global climate, covering 1950 to the present.

Source: Asian Development Bank project team and consultant experts, using data from ERA5 (drought and extreme low temperature).

Table 3.3: Changes in Future Climate under Medium and High Emissions Scenarios (Khiva)

Variable	Units [Δ units]	Historic	Δ RCP45 2030	Δ RCP45 2050	Δ RCP85 2030	Δ RCP85 2050
Average climate trends						
Mean Annual Temperature	°C [°C]	20.1	1.3	2	1.5	2.6
			[0.7, 1.9]	[1.5, 2.6]	[0.9, 2.1]	[1.8, 3.3]
Total Annual Precipitation	mm/year [%]	65.9	10.3	8.5	2.6	6.2
			[(12.5), 35.5]	[(14.3), 34.9]	[(19.4), 31.1]	[(18.5), 31]
Extreme temperature trends						
Maximum Annual Temperature	°C [°C]	41	1.5	2.2	1.5	2.9
			[0.6, 2.5]	[1.3, 3.1]	[0.7, 2.8]	[2, 4]
Minimum Annual Temperature	°C [°C]	(16.3)	2	2.3	2	3.1
			[(1.4), 4.4]	[(0.8), 4.9]	[(1.1), 4.5]	[(0.2), 5.5]
Extreme precipitation trends						
Maximum 1-Day Precipitation	mm/day [%]	10.3	3.7	6.9	3.1	5.1
			[(26), 38.1]	[(21.4), 42.4]	[(24.8), 34.1]	[(22.9), 35.2]
Drought Period Length	days [days]	185.5	(4.1)	(1.2)	(0.2)	1
			[(16.7), 12.7]	[(15.7), 11.9]	[(15.1), 17.3]	[(13.2), 18.2]

Δ = change, ( ) = negative, mm = millimeter, RCP = representative concentration pathway.

Notes: Numbers in brackets represent median values (25th percentile, 75th percentile) of climate model ensemble predictions.
ERA5 refers to the 5th generation atmospheric reanalysis of the global climate, covering 1950 to the present.

Source: Asian Development Bank project team and consultant experts, using data from ERA5 (historical) and NASA Earth Exchange climate model projections (RCP45 and RCP85).

Figure 3.9: Return Period Analysis of Extreme Precipitation Events (Khiva)

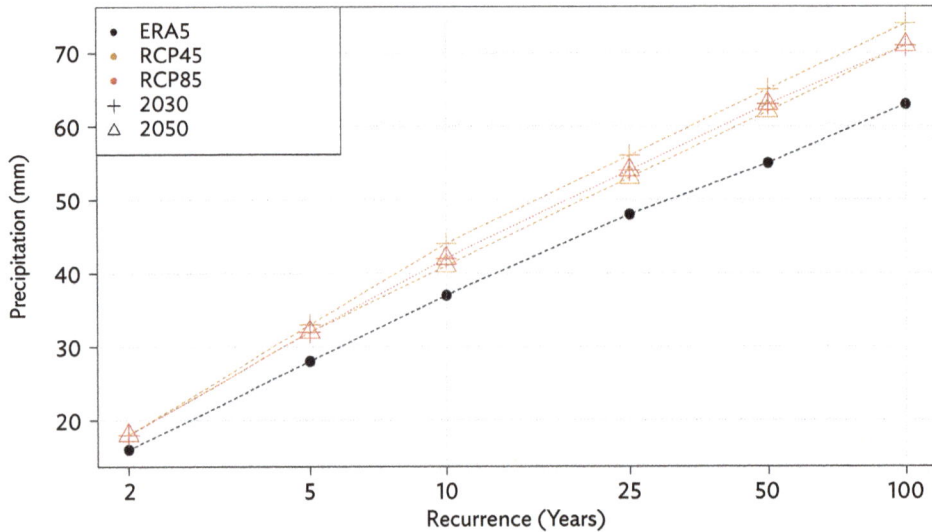

	Return Period					
	2 Years	5 Years	10 Years	25 Years	50 Years	100 Years
Historical daily maximum precipitation (mm)						
ERA5	16	28	37	48	55	63
Future (75th percentile of GCM distribution) (mm)						
RCP45 2030	18	33	44	56	65	74
RCP45 2050	18	32	41	53	62	71
RCP85 2030	18	32	42	54	63	71
RCP85 2050	18	32	42	54	63	71

Δ = change, GCM = global circulation model, mm = millimeter, RCP = representative concentration pathway.

Notes: The analysis represents changes in the yearly maximum 1-day precipitation (Rx1day) at various return periods, providing predictions of future frequencies of extreme precipitation events. It is based on the third quartile (75th percentile) of ensemble predictions and uses a Gumbel fitting approach to estimate the extreme events. The numbers can be used to inform the design of more climate-resilient urban infrastructure.

ERA5 refers to the 5th generation atmospheric reanalysis of the global climate, covering 1950 to the present.

Source: Asian Development Bank project team and consultant experts, using data from ERA5 (historical) and NASA Earth Exchange climate model projections (RCP45 and RCP85).

3.4 Climate Trends and Risk Analyses: Yangiyer (Sirdaryo Province)

SUMMARY (2050)

City-scale risk
- Moderate risk of extreme heat, concentrated in urban areas
- High flood risk in urban areas and along roads

National-scale hazards
- Likely to experience water stress problems
- Area likely to be frequently exposed to extreme cold events

Changes in climate
- Moderate increases in maximum yearly temperature increasing frequency and intensity of heat waves
- Large increases in maximum 1-day precipitation events may increase flood risk

Extreme precipitation
- The most severe precipitation events predicted by climate model ensemble are of moderate intensity

Figure 3.10: Current Risk Associated with Extreme Heat and Riverine Flooding (Yangiyer)

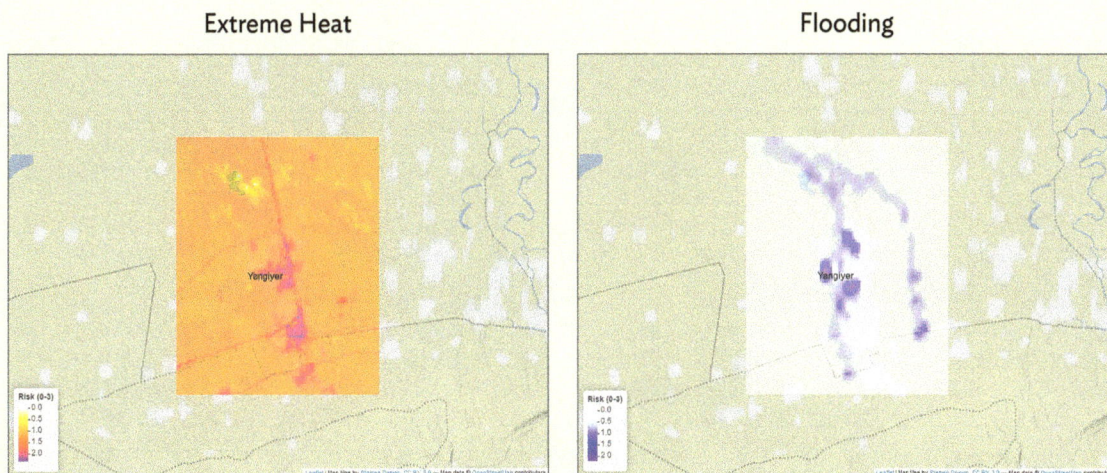

Extreme Heat

Flooding

Note: 0 = no risk, 3 = high risk.

Source: Asian Development Bank project team and consultant experts, using data from the United Nations (population density and gross domestic product); OpenStreetMap (vulnerability of road networks, buildings, and points of interest); United Nations Office for Disaster Risk Reduction. 2015. *Global Assessment Report on Disaster Risk Reduction 2015*. Geneva (1 in 100-year flood hazard); and Google Earth Engine (heat anomaly signals).

Figure 3.11: Current Hazards Associated with Water Shortage or Drought and Extreme Cold Events (Yangiyer)

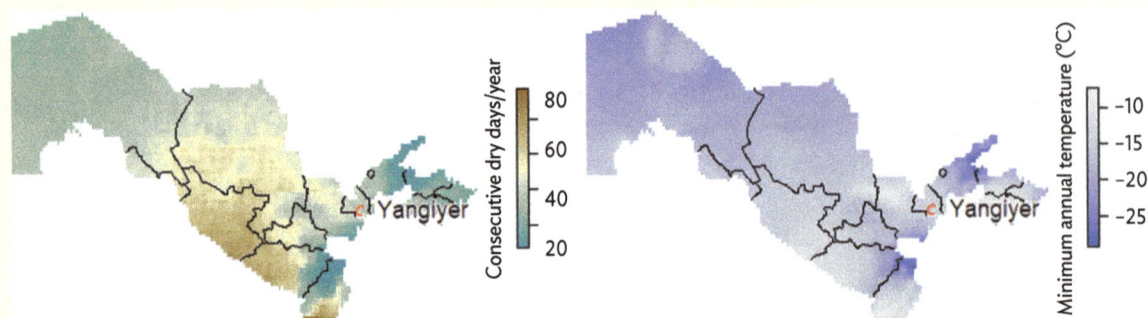

Notes: Map shows the spatial distribution of each hazard and the location of the urban area in this context.
        ERA5 refers to the 5th generation atmospheric reanalysis of the global climate, covering 1950 to the present.

Source: Asian Development Bank project team and consultant experts, using data from ERA5 (drought and extreme low temperature).

Table 3.4: Changes in Future Climate under Medium and High Emissions Scenarios (Yangiyer)

Variable	Units [Δ units]	Historic	Δ RCP45 2030	Δ RCP45 2050	Δ RCP85 2030	Δ RCP85 2050
Average climate trends						
Mean Annual Temperature	°C [°C]	21.6	**1.3** [0.8, 1.9]	**2** ([1.4, 2.7]	**1.6** [1, 2]	**2.6** [1.9, 3.5]
Total Annual Precipitation	mm/year [%]	366.7	**5.7** [(9.20), 23.3]	**4.9** [(14.3), 24.5]	**1.7** [(15.8), 21.3]	**3.2** [(14.5), 25.8]
Extreme temperature trends						
Maximum Annual Temperature	°C [°C]	40.4	**1.5** [0.6, 2.5]	**2.3** [1.5, 3.3]	**1.8** [0.8, 3]	**3.1** [2.1, 4.2]
Minimum Annual Temperature	°C [°C]	(11.7)	**1.7** [(0.8), 4]	**2.2** [(0.4), 4.8]	**2.1** [(0.5), 4.5]	**2.8** [0.5, 5.4]
Extreme precipitation trends						
Maximum 1-Day Precipitation	mm/day [%]	28	**6.9** [(17.8), 35.2]	**12.6** [(15.7), 42.2]	**9.8** [(17.5), 42.7]	**15.1** [(11.3), 48.8]
Drought Period Length	days [days]	123.7	**2.5** [(9), 15.7]	**2.5** [(7.7), 13.3]	**1.6** [(9.5), 15.3]	**5.5** [(5.3), 18.7]

Δ = change, ( ) = negative, mm = millimeter, RCP = representative concentration pathway.

Notes: Numbers in brackets represent median values (25th percentile, 75th percentile) of climate model ensemble predictions.
        ERA5 refers to the 5th generation atmospheric reanalysis of the global climate, covering 1950 to the present.

Source: Asian Development Bank project team and consultant experts, using data from ERA5 (historical) and NASA Earth Exchange climate model projections (RCP45 and RCP85).

Figure 3.12: Return Period Analysis of Extreme Precipitation Events (Yangiyer)

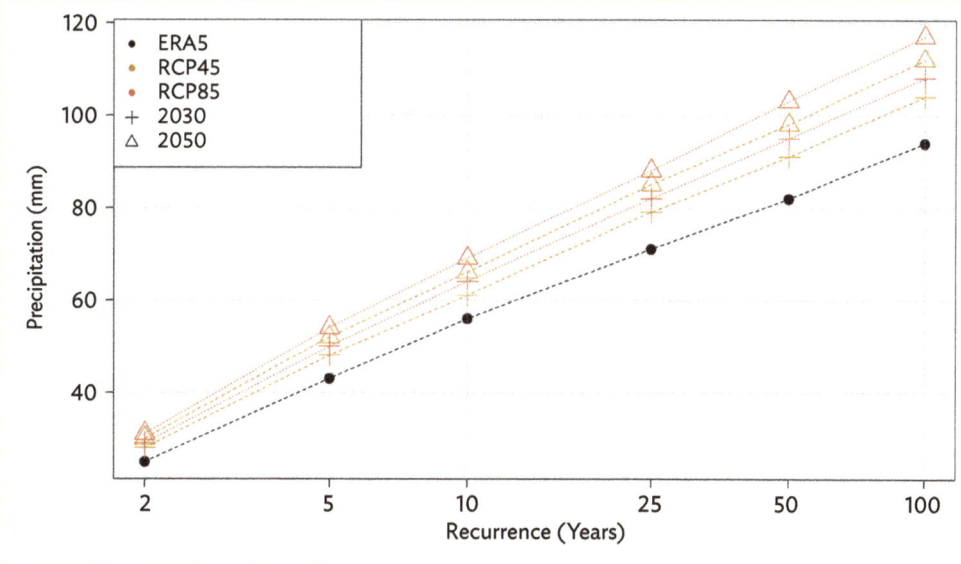

	Return Period					
	2 Years	5 Years	10 Years	25 Years	50 Years	100 Years
Historical daily maximum precipitation (mm)						
ERA5	25	43	56	71	82	94
Future (75th percentile of GCM distribution) (mm)						
RCP45 2030	28	48	61	79	91	104
RCP45 2050	30	52	66	85	98	112
RCP85 2030	29	50	64	82	95	108
RCP85 2050	31	54	69	88	103	117

Δ = change, GCM = global circulation model, mm = millimeter, RCP = representative concentration pathway.

Notes: The analysis represents changes in the yearly maximum 1-day precipitation (Rx1day) at various return periods, providing predictions of future frequencies of extreme precipitation events. It is based on the third quartile (75th percentile) of ensemble predictions and uses a Gumbel fitting approach to estimate the extreme events. The numbers can be used to inform the design of more climate-resilient urban infrastructure.

ERA5 refers to the 5th generation atmospheric reanalysis of the global climate, covering 1950 to the present.

Source: Asian Development Bank project team and consultant experts, using data from ERA5 (historical) and NASA Earth Exchange climate model projections (RCP45 and RCP85).

3.5 Climate Trends and Risk Analyses: Tashkent

SUMMARY (2050)

City-scale risk
- High risk of extreme heat, concentrated in urban center
- Areas of moderate flood risk, in urban areas and along roads

National-scale hazards
- Likely to experience water stress problems
- Area likely frequently exposed to extreme cold events

Changes in climate
- Moderate increases in maximum yearly temperature increasing frequency and intensity of heat waves
- Moderate increases in maximum 1-day precipitation events may increase flood risk

Extreme precipitation
- The most severe precipitation events predicted by climate model ensemble are of moderate intensity

Figure 3.13: Current Risk Associated with Extreme Heat and Riverine Flooding (Tashkent)

Extreme Heat

Flooding

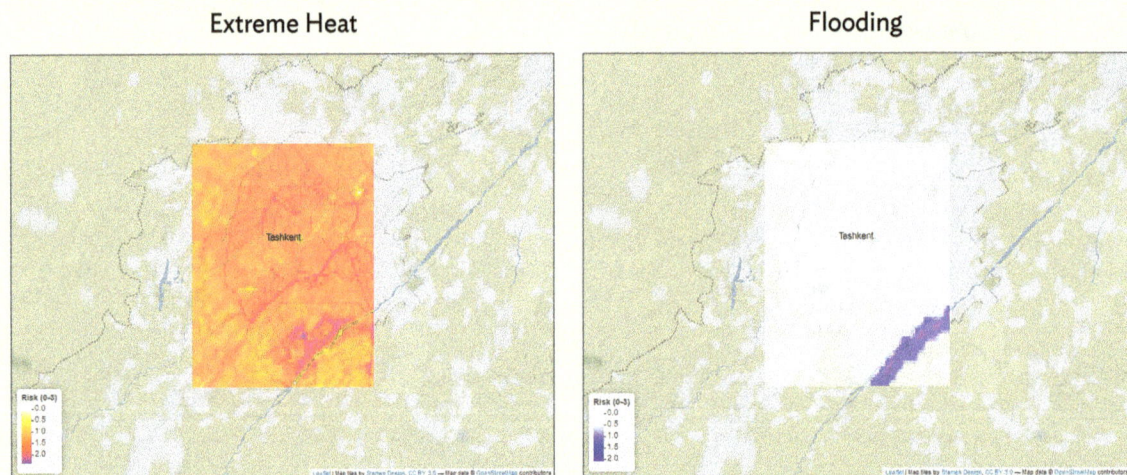

Note: 0 = no risk, 3 = high risk.

Source: Asian Development Bank project team and consultant experts, using data from the United Nations (population density and gross domestic product); OpenStreetMap (vulnerability of road networks, buildings, and points of interest); United Nations Office for Disaster Risk Reduction. 2015. *Global Assessment Report on Disaster Risk Reduction 2015*. Geneva (1 in 100-year flood hazard); and Google Earth Engine (heat anomaly signals).

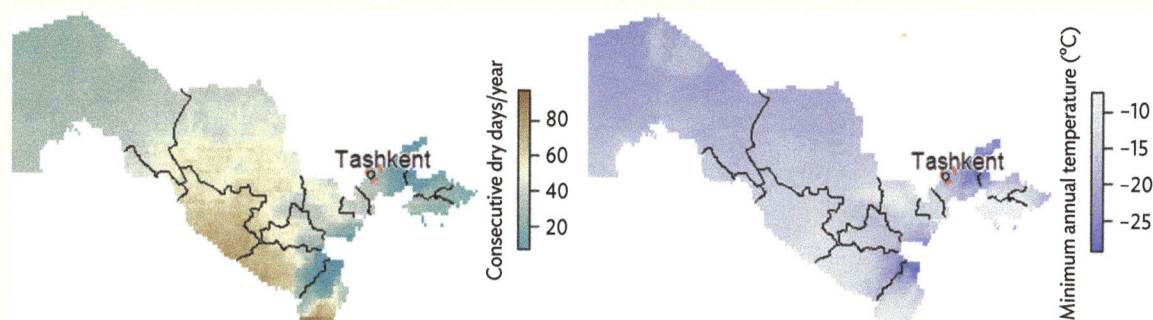

Figure 3.14: Current Hazards Associated with Water Shortage or Drought and Extreme Cold Events (Tashkent)

Notes: Map shows the spatial distribution of each hazard and the location of the urban area in this context.
ERA5 refers to the 5th generation atmospheric reanalysis of the global climate, covering 1950 to the present.

Source: Asian Development Bank project team and consultant experts, using data from ERA5 (drought and extreme low temperature).

Table 3.5: Changes in Future Climate under Medium and High Emissions Scenarios (Tashkent)

Variable	Units [Δ units]	Historic	Δ RCP45 2030	Δ RCP45 2050	Δ RCP85 2030	Δ RCP85 2050
Average climate trends						
Mean Annual Temperature	°C [°C]	20.3	1.4 [0.8, 2]	2 [1.5, 2.8]	1.6 [1, 2.1]	2.6 [2, 3.5]
Total Annual Precipitation	mm/year [%]	401.9	6.2 [(10.6), 23.1]	4.1 [(14.5), 26.1]	1.4 [(17.7), 20.9]	3.6 [(11.5), 25.2]
Extreme temperature trends						
Maximum Annual Temperature	°C [°C]	39.3	1.6 [0.8, 2.6]	2.4 [1.6, 3.4]	1.9 [0.9, 3.1]	3.1 [2.3, 4.1]
Minimum Annual Temperature	°C [°C]	(13.2)	2 [(0.7), 4.4]	2.4 [(0.1), 5.1]	2.2 [(0.5), 4.4]	3.2 [0.6, 5.7]
Extreme precipitation trends						
Maximum 1-Day Precipitation	mm/day [%]	29	3.9 [(16.7), 36.1]	9.4 [(15), 42.3]	8 [(19.7), 46.6]	12.6 [(15.3), 51.1]
Drought Period Length	days [days]	114.3	1 [(11.7), 16.7]	2.7 [(10), 16]	1.7 [(10.7), 19.3]	5.7 [(8.7), 20.7]

Δ = change, ( ) = negative, mm = millimeter, RCP = representative concentration pathway.

Notes: Numbers in brackets represent median values (25th percentile, 75th percentile) of climate model ensemble predictions.
ERA5 refers to the 5th generation atmospheric reanalysis of the global climate, covering 1950 to the present.

Source: Asian Development Bank project team and consultant experts, using data from ERA5 (historical) and NASA Earth Exchange climate model projections (RCP45 and RCP85).

Figure 3.15: Return Period Analysis of Extreme Precipitation Events (Tashkent)

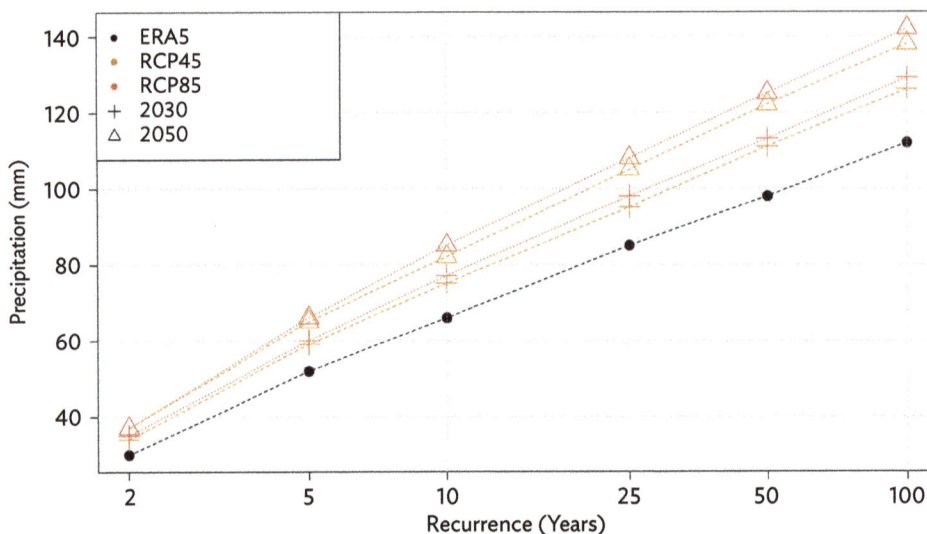

	Return Period					
	2 Years	5 Years	10 Years	25 Years	50 Years	100 Years
Historical daily maximum precipitation (mm)						
ERA5	30	52	66	85	98	112
Future (75th percentile of GCM distribution) (mm)						
RCP45 2030	34	59	75	95	111	126
RCP45 2050	37	65	82	105	122	138
RCP85 2030	35	60	77	98	113	129
RCP85 2050	37	66	85	108	125	142

Δ = change, GCM = global circulation model, mm = millimeter, RCP = representative concentration pathway.

Notes: The analysis represents changes in the yearly maximum 1-day precipitation (Rx1day) at various return periods, providing predictions of future frequencies of extreme precipitation events. It is based on the third quartile (75th percentile) of ensemble predictions and uses a Gumbel fitting approach to estimate the extreme events. The numbers can be used to inform the design of more climate-resilient urban infrastructure.

ERA5 refers to the 5th generation atmospheric reanalysis of the global climate, covering 1950 to the present.

Source: Asian Development Bank project team and consultant experts, using data from ERA5 (historical) and NASA Earth Exchange climate model projections (RCP45 and RCP85).

3.6 Options for Mainstreaming Climate Change in Urban Planning

Key Considerations in Selected Subsectors

Adaptation starts at the planning stage. Taking climate change risks into account in both land-use planning and siting of infrastructure is of paramount importance, as is answering questions such as "Which infrastructure projects are needed to enhance urban climate resilience?" And "Is this project appropriate within the urban risk context?"

Table 3.6 provides some specific measures that may be considered in the planning process at the national level. The focus of this table is on key subsectors that may be affected by climate change and correspond to priority areas of ADB investment. Health and energy, although relevant, are beyond the scope of this profile.

Table 3.6: Planning Considerations for Selected Urban Subsectors

Projected Climate Change	Relevance to Area (Low/Medium/High)[a]	Potential Impacts on Infrastructure	Possible Planning Considerations and/or Actions
Transport Infrastructure			
Small to moderate increases in precipitation intensity, maximum 1-day precipitation events	Medium Issue along large river channels (Amu Darya), eastern provinces with steep topography and more intense precipitation	Increased precipitation potentially leading to increased damage to roads and transport infrastructure due to floods, mudslides, landslides, and avalanches	• Account for flooding risks in decisions regarding the siting of roads and rails and related transport infrastructure • Incorporate blue spaces and green spaces in planning to cope with excess water • Encourage mixed-use, vertical, and compact development as opposed to urban sprawl to reduce dependence on car-driven lifestyles
Moderate increase in maximum temperatures and frequency of heat waves	High High extreme heat signal nationwide, especially in eastern provinces, urban centers	Intense heat waves and increased temperatures potentially affecting transport infrastructure and requiring more frequent repairs, as well as affecting users	Include nature-based solutions in planning to reduce the urban heat island effect, e.g., tree planting, creation of urban water bodies and green roofs[b]
Moderate increase in minimum yearly temperatures, considerable decrease in frost days	Medium Extreme low temperatures likely to still occur in all areas	Increases in minimum temperatures potentially leading to a decrease in frost- and ice-related damage to infrastructure	No adaptation needed to address climate change risks, possibly a gain to be realized from climate change

continued on next page

Table 3.6 *continued*

Projected Climate Change	Relevance to Area (Low/Medium/High)[a]	Potential Impacts on Infrastructure	Possible Planning Considerations and/or Actions
Buildings			
Small to moderate increases in precipitation intensity, maximum 1-day precipitation events	Medium Issue along large river channels (Amu Darya), eastern provinces with steep topography and more intense precipitation	Increased precipitation potentially leading to increased damage to buildings due to floods, mudslides, landslides, and avalanches	• Climate-informed land-use planning (e.g., siting of buildings) • Climate-resilient building codes • Upgrading of existing surface water management and drainage infrastructure for increased intensity precipitation events • Incorporation of SUDSs in planning process • Early warning systems[c]
Moderate increase in maximum temperatures and frequency of heat waves	High High extreme heat signal nationally, especially in eastern provinces, urban centers	Intense heat waves and increased temperatures potentially affecting buildings and users	• Building guidelines to improve temperature regulation in buildings and encourage the use of heat-resistant materials • Green-blue infrastructure such as urban green space, water features, green roofs, and shading trees
Moderate increase in minimum yearly temperatures, considerable decrease in frost days	Medium Extreme low temperatures still likely to occur in all areas	Increases in minimum temperatures potentially leading to a decrease in frost- and ice-related damage to buildings	• No adaptation needed to address climate change risks, possibly a gain from climate change to be realized • Incorporate climate risk management and adaptation in government infrastructure projects[d]
Sanitation, Sewerage, and Water Supply			
Moderate increases in precipitation intensity, maximum 1-day precipitation events	Low Low precipitation nationwide, but this is likely to be more of an issue in eastern provinces where precipitation is higher and more intense	Increased extreme precipitation events may exceed urban water cycle capacity	• Enhance land-use planning, focusing on increasing percentage of permeable and semipermeable green space and creating water storage and retention in urban areas[e] • Upgrade capacity of sewerage networks • Incorporate SUDSs in drainage planning • Develop and implement climate-resilient drainage and wastewater management plans
Decrease or small increase in drought length, decrease or small increase in total precipitation	High Intensity of drought may decrease, but frequency may not; western provinces are very drought prone	Increased intensity of droughts may cause water shortages	• Measures to increase water efficiency (loss reduction) in infrastructure • Demand management measures[f] • Diversification of water supply, water recycling, and use of alternative water resources[g] • Drought management and early warning strategies

continued on next page

Table 3.6 *continued*

Projected Climate Change	Relevance to Area (Low/Medium/High)[a]	Potential Impacts on Infrastructure	Possible Planning Considerations and/or Actions
Solid Waste			
Moderate increase in maximum annual temperatures	**Medium** This is likely to be more of an issue in eastern provinces where the temperature is less extreme	Increased temperature may require an improvement of the waste management system to cope with potentially increased risks of pathogenic germs to health	• 3Rs (reduce, reuse, and recycle) awareness raising and waste minimization campaigns • Upgrading of landfill sites to avoid mobilization of pollutants and reduce methane emissions

NDC = nationally determined contribution, SUDS = sustainable urban drainage system.

[a] Relevance ratings are determined by expert judgment based on relevant datasets presented in the climate risk profiles.

[b] More guidance may be obtained from J. Matthews and E. O. Dela Cruz. 2022. *Integrating Nature-Based Solutions for Climate Change Adaptation and Disaster Risk Management: A Practitioner's Guide.* Manila: ADB.

[c] In its latest NDC update, Uzbekistan identifies the development of early warning systems on hydrometeorological hazards as an adaptation measure it will complete by 2030, especially to manage climate risks in the social sphere. Government of Uzbekistan. 2021. *Republic of Uzbekistan: Updated Nationally Determined Contribution 2021.* Tashkent.

[d] This is supported by Uzbekistan's updated NDC, which includes the introduction of "adaptation criteria into public investment projects for construction, modernization, operation and maintenance of infrastructure in various sectors of the economy" in the adaptation measures to be undertaken by the country through 2030. Government of Uzbekistan. 2021. *Republic of Uzbekistan: Updated Nationally Determined Contribution 2021.* Tashkent. p. 24.

[e] See the "sponge city" concept piloted in several cities in the People's Republic of China with support from ADB. ADB. 2017. Piloting "Sponge Cities" in the People's Republic of China. Project result/case study. 13 January.

[f] This includes a variety of measures including tariffs, pricing, user controls, awareness raising, and smart network monitoring.

[g] Technologies exist that can use brackish water or wastewater as inputs and produce a combination of food (aquaculture products, vegetables, animal feed) and clean water. Applicability for Uzbekistan would need to be assessed. The advantage of such technology is that it involves an ecosystem-based approach in line with Uzbekistan's NDC.

Source: Asian Development Bank project team.

Considerations on Enabling Environment, Local Government Planning, and Operation and Maintenance

Early action on other key considerations relating to planning and O&M can accelerate urban climate resiliency building in Uzbekistan. Some of these considerations are presented below.

Enabling environment for climate resilience planning

The central government can consider the following measures:

- Ensure that local governments and stakeholders are equipped with adequate data, information, and skills that will help them to respond to the impacts of climate change. This could be in the form of data portals and knowledge-sharing workshops.

- Ensure that cities coping with climate change have sufficient access to finance, for example, by providing access to international climate finance through applications by the central government to financing sources such as the Green Climate Fund.

- Ensure that individuals and communities affected by climate change-related hazards can recover and rebuild as quickly as possible via access to insurance and national government support programs.

- Develop building codes and standards for infrastructure that consider changes in climate, such as new flood return periods.

- Introduce and institutionalize risk-based land use and open space planning. Introduce blue-green resilience networks and nature-based solutions as a first step in all spatial planning.
- Initiate and sustain benchmarking and monitoring of efforts across cities and local government jurisdictions, facilitating knowledge transfer between these parties.

Local government planning

Local governments may wish to incorporate the following task items in their planning process:

- Consider how expected climate change interacts with the cities' development visions and how expected climate change may impact the relative viability of investments. This is especially important to determine the performance of built assets over their respective project life cycles.
- Develop climate hazard maps to guide urban development, e.g., to integrate flood risks in urban spatial planning. This requires local-scale, higher-resolution modeling to better map the influence on hazards of a full envelope of likely changes in climate.
- Ensure that individuals and communities at risk to climate-related hazards are aware of the risks they are exposed to and how these may change in the future. This could be achieved via community outreach.
- Climate hazard information should be factored into the design and implementation of development regulation instruments, such as zoning, land subdivision, and building codes. This will help reduce climate change vulnerability and avoid the expansion of development to high-risk areas.
- Adopt, implement, and enforce building codes and standards for infrastructure that take account of changes in climate, such as new flood return periods.
- Promote the development of early warning systems and climate change-related disaster response strategies (often as part of a more comprehensive disaster response strategy).
- Initiate community-level education programs for disaster preparedness. These should focus on preparing communities for situations where authorities and emergency services are unable to access affected areas to provide critical assistance in the aftermath of a disaster.
- Undertake institutional strengthening for climate action through reform of responsibilities and creation of a high-level climate change office under the governor and mayor and cross-departmental working groups.

Operation and maintenance

Adequate O&M is as important as up-front capital investments in ensuring climate-resilient infrastructure and physical assets. The following section details some key considerations relating to O&M:

- Ensure that risk-informed O&M is considered from the earliest stages of planning and design for new infrastructure projects.
- Update existing O&M plans to reflect changes in precipitation and temperature, which may necessitate more frequent maintenance or changes in operational practices.
- Create backup emergency infrastructure in case of failure in key infrastructure, e.g., the maintenance of emergency generators in case of power failure.

- Ensure regular inspection and maintenance of infrastructure relating to hazard protection, e.g., flood protection structures.

- Implement smart monitoring strategies and the Internet of Things to collect, centralize, and review data relating to hydrometeorology and key infrastructure.

- Implement risk informed preventive maintenance, which may be a highly feasible and cost-effective approach for ensuring overall network resilience.

- Prioritize O&M of telecommunication networks, which play a critical role in disaster response efforts.

Under the Integrated Urban Development Project, ADB is helping the Government of Uzbekistan enhance the climate resilience and livability of Khiva, a popular tourist destination, for both its residents and visitors (photo by Relisa Granovskaya/ADB).

3.7 Infrastructure Design Considerations

Table 3.7 provides some key considerations for the design and/or upgrading of urban infrastructure assets to enhance climate resilience based on expert judgment of climate model ensemble outputs, including possible adaptation measures. The focus of this table is on key urban subsectors that may be affected by climate change and correspond to priority areas of ADB investment. While potentially relevant, the health and energy sectors are beyond the scope of this profile.

Table 3.7: Design Considerations for Urban Infrastructure in Selected Cities

Projected Climate Change	Relevance to Area (Low/Medium/High)					Potential Impacts on Infrastructure	Possible Adaptation Measures
	Djizzak	Khiva	Yangiyer	Tashkent		Djizzak, Khiva, Yangiyer, Tashkent	
Transport Infrastructure							
Relatively large increases in precipitation intensity, maximum 1-day precipitation events	Medium Limited riverine flood risk in city center, mostly along road networks outside city	Low Limited areas at risk of riverine flooding in urban center	High High riverine flood risk along main roads, in urban center	Medium Some riverine flood risk to southeast of the city center		Increased precipitation potentially leading to increased damage to roads and transport infrastructure due to floods, mudslides, landslides, and avalanches	• Enhance drainage • Reinforce vulnerable structures • Utilize permeable road and pavements • Increase the height and setback of flood defenses and dikes
Moderate increase in maximum temperatures and frequency of heat waves	High Risk concentrated in urban centers			High Risk concentrated in large urban center, airport to the south may be affected		Intense heat waves and increased temperatures potentially affecting transport infrastructure and requiring more frequent repairs, as well as affecting users	• Use road construction materials that are more resistant to heat[a] • Use road construction materials with self-healing properties[b] • Plant trees along roadsides • Enhance ventilation and cooling for public transport systems
Moderate increase in minimum yearly temperatures, considerable decrease in frost days	Medium Extreme low temperatures will likely still occur		Medium Extreme low temperatures will be less frequent, especially in urban areas	Medium Extreme low temperatures will be less frequent, even less so in warm city center		Increases in minimum temperatures potentially leading to a decrease in frost- and ice-related damage to infrastructure	No adaptation needed to address climate change risks, possibly a gain from climate change

continued on next page

Table 3.7 *continued*

Projected Climate Change	Relevance to Area (Low/Medium/High)				Potential Impacts on Infrastructure	Possible Adaptation Measures
	Djizzak	Khiva	Yangiyer	Tashkent	Djizzak, Khiva, Yangiyer, Tashkent	
Buildings						
Moderate increases in precipitation intensity, maximum 1-day precipitation events	Low – Limited riverine flood risk in city center, low likelihood of landslide or mudslide	Low – Limited areas at risk of riverine flooding in urban center	High – High riverine flood risk in urban center	Medium – Some riverine flood risk to the southeast of city center	Increased precipitation potentially leading to increased damage to buildings due to floods, mudslides, landslides, and avalanches	• Enhance drainage infrastructure to cope with increased intensity precipitation events • Install SUDSs, e.g., retention basins, bioswales • Stream or river daylighting, floodplain restoration • Protective infrastructure such as flood barriers, slope stabilization measures, and dams • Bracing technologies against strong winds
Moderate increase in maximum temperatures and frequency of heat waves	High – Risk concentrated in urban center	High – High extreme heat signal, concentrated in urban center	High – Risk concentrated in urban center	High – Risk concentrated in large urban center, extreme in area to the south of city center	Intense heat waves and increased temperatures potentially affecting buildings and users	• White roofs • Green roofs and shading trees • Airtight sealing and double-glazing of glass windows and doors • Increased thermal mass of buildings • Use of heat-reflective materials to minimize solar heat gain • Ensured ventilation • Efficient cooling[c]
Moderate increase in minimum yearly temperatures, considerable decrease in frost days	Medium – Extreme low temperatures will likely still occur		Medium – Extreme low temperatures will be less frequent, especially in urban areas	Medium – Extreme low temperatures will be less frequent, even less so in warm city center	Increases in minimum temperatures potentially leading to a decrease in frost- and ice-related damage to buildings	No adaptation needed to address climate change risks, possibly a gain from climate change to be realized

continued on next page

Table 3.7 *continued*

Projected Climate Change	Relevance to Area (Low/Medium/High)				Potential Impacts on Infrastructure	Possible Adaptation Measures
	Djizzak	Khiva	Yangiyer	Tashkent	Djizzak, Khiva, Yangiyer, Tashkent	Djizzak, Khiva, Yangiyer, Tashkent
Sanitation, Sewerage, and Water Supply						
Moderate increases in precipitation intensity, maximum 1-day precipitation events	Medium	Low Although predicted to increase, precipitation events will remain irregular and mild in intensity	High	Medium Risk may be aggravated by complexities due to size of city	Increased extreme precipitation events may exceed urban water cycle capacity	• Upgrade drainage and/or sewerage assets to increase capacity for high-intensity precipitation events • Install SUDSs e.g., bioswales, retention basins. • Consider separating stormwater and wastewater • Build treatment wetlands to support wastewater treatment infrastructure
Decrease or very small increase in drought length, increase in total precipitation	Medium Intensity may decrease, but frequency may not; already a drought-prone area		Medium Already a drought-prone area	Medium Already a drought-prone area; may be aggravated by complexities due to size of city	Potentially increased intensity of droughts may cause water shortages	• Diversify water sources: groundwater and surface water • Reuse and recycle water • Harvest rainwater • Reuse wastewater for agricultural irrigation and industrial purposes
Solid Waste						
Moderate increase in maximum annual temperatures	Medium May be problematic in urban center	Low Temperature extremes in the area make this less relevant	Medium May be problematic in urban centers		Increased temperature may require an improvement of the waste management system to cope with potentially increased risks of pathogenic germs to health	• Enhance waste collection, storage, and processing as appropriate • Waste collection and treatment could include a combination of recycling and reuse, anaerobic digestion, and incineration[d]

SUDS = sustainable urban drainage system.

[a] Examples include warm-mix asphalt and engineered cementitious composites.

[b] Materials with self-healing properties are those that automatically fill cracks without human intervention. Different materials (including concretes based on pozzolanic materials, concretes based on cements with added bacteria, and concrete with special coatings) can exhibit this behavior and may be used for road and bridge construction.

[c] Through the use of (i) efficient air conditioners with low global warming potential refrigerants, efficient chillers, and trigeneration technologies; and (ii) information technology to support energy efficiency in buildings using existing assets. Solution (ii) can be a low-cost option with a short payback period. It could also be considered a mitigation strategy as well as an adaptation measure. In specific locations, heat pumps could be used using river water as a source of cooling.

[d] Effective, commercially viable technologies exist for anaerobic digestion of waste and incineration for the generation of zero-emission power. Promotion of such technologies could be considered a mitigation strategy as well as an adaptation measure.

Source: Asian Development Bank project team.

GUIDANCE ON INTERPRETING THE CLIMATE RISK PROFILES

SUMMARY

The risk profiles can be used to
- Generate a broad understanding of potential future changes in climate
- Understand large-scale (national and regional) future changes in climate
- Generate a range of future scenarios to be considered in planning
- Identify hotspots where flooding or extreme heat could pose problems to existing infrastructure or development

They cannot be used to
- Predict exact changes in climate variables over time
- Understand street- and city-scale spatial patterns in climate change
- Guide local (street-level) development decisions
- Remove the need for detailed local risk-scoping studies

How the Climate Risk Profiles Should Be Used

Users of the national and urban climate risk profiles presented in this publication are advised to consider the uncertainties and limitations of the climate data for downstream work. When using the outputs to understand climate change at a national or regional level, it would be best to consider these outputs in broad terms and avoid focusing on specific values. For example, to determine how mean annual precipitation is likely to change, it would be more appropriate to consider a range of model projections, rather than simply focusing on the median predicted change. For this purpose, the use of the 25th and 75th percentiles in the risk profiles will continue to be valuable.

For decisions relating to planning and development in which it is difficult to incorporate a range of model projections, it is recommended that the worst-case scenario be planned for. This worst-case scenario corresponds to the extreme percentile of model outputs for the RCP85 scenario. For example, when preparing for changes in extreme heat waves and their effects on a national to regional scale, the change projected as the 75th percentile of model outputs for the RCP85 scenario should be considered. This approach is important to promote resilience in planning, however clear the trade-offs may be between safety (or risk aversion) and the amount of resources needed to prepare for a given future.

Limitations

The risk profiles presented here are based on analyses of downscaled climate models of different future scenarios. They aim to identify considerations that may be relevant for climate-resilient urban development. But as the profiles do not provide a comprehensive picture of all the risks and possible adaptation measures, it is crucial for the central government and urban focal agencies to inform their investment decisions with additional rigorous, context-specific analyses, and more detailed, up-to-date data from stakeholder consultations, as well as more granular engineering and hydrological surveys. Topics that are not touched upon here, but should be considered, include (i) adaptation measures that may be undertaken across infrastructure systems, including consideration of users or beneficiaries, governance, environment, resources, and existing infrastructure assets; and (ii) interdependence between multi-hazards and different subsectors.

The overview offered in the risk profiles focuses mainly on climate change-related hazards. The need to consider vulnerability and exposure to fully characterize future changes in risk cannot be overemphasized. These factors are representative of (i) the resilience of communities and infrastructure to hazards, and (ii) the changing nature of where people live and assets are constructed. Factor (ii) is especially important, as populations globally continue to expand into hazard-prone areas such as floodplains. As such, the largest changes in risk in many areas may be because of exposure changes rather than climate change-induced exacerbation of hazards. It is therefore suggested that urban population growth and development trends be spatially analyzed and compared with these hazard maps to characterize future risk more accurately.

REFERENCES

Asian Development Bank (ADB). 2016. *Realizing the Urban Potential in Georgia: National Urban Assessment*. Manila.

ADB. 2017a. Piloting "Sponge Cities" in the People's Republic of China. Project result/case study. 13 January.

———. 2017b. *Climate Change Operational Framework, 2017–2030: Enhanced Actions for Low Greenhouse Gas Emissions and Climate-Resilient Development*. Manila.

———. 2018. *Strategy 2030: Achieving a Prosperous, Inclusive, Resilient, and Sustainable Asia and the Pacific*. Manila.

———. 2019a. *Technical Assistance for Supporting the Implementation of ADB's Climate Change Operational Framework 2017–2030—Subproject 1: Supporting Ambitious Climate Action through Implementation of Developing Member Countries' Nationally Determined Contributions*. Manila.

———. 2019b. *Armenia's Transformative Urban Future: National Urban Assessment*. Manila.

———. 2021. *Harnessing Uzbekistan's Potential of Urbanization: National Urban Assessment*. Manila.

———. 2022. *NDC Advance: Accelerating Climate Actions in Asia and the Pacific*. Manila.

Government of Armenia. 2015. *Intended Nationally Determined Contributions of the Republic of Armenia under the United Nations Framework Convention on Climate Change*. Yerevan.

———. 2020. *Fourth National Communication on Climate Change under the United Nations Convention on Climate Change*. Yerevan.

———. 2021. *Nationally Determined Contribution 2021–2030 of the Republic of Armenia to the Paris Agreement*. Yerevan.

Government of Uzbekistan. 2015. *Intended Nationally Determined Contributions of the Republic of Uzbekistan*. Tashkent.

———. 2021. Republic of Uzbekistan. *Updated Nationally Determined Contribution 2021*. Tashkent.

Lu, X. 2019. Building Resilient Infrastructure for the Future: Background paper for the G20 Climate Sustainability Working Group. *ADB Sustainable Development Working Paper Series*. No. 61. Manila: ADB.

Matthews, J., and E. O. Dela Cruz. 2022. *Integrating Nature-Based Solutions for Climate Change Adaptation and Disaster Risk Management: A Practitioner's Guide.* Manila: ADB.

United Nations Office for Disaster Risk Reduction. 2015. *Global Assessment Report on Disaster Risk Reduction 2015.* Geneva.

www.ingramcontent.com/pod-product-compliance
Lightning Source LLC
Chambersburg PA
CBHW050047220326
41599CB00045B/7313